Certain Security

Certain Security

Finding Refuge from Criminal, Economic, and Political Instability through US Investment Visas

Brian Dickens

iUniverse, Inc.
Bloomington

CERTAIN SECURITY
FINDING REFUGE FROM CRIMINAL, ECONOMIC, AND POLITICAL INSTABILITY THROUGH US INVESTMENT VISAS

Copyright © 2013 Brian Dickens.

All rights reserved. No part of this book may be used or reproduced by any means, graphic, electronic, or mechanical, including photocopying, recording, taping or by any information storage retrieval system without the written permission of the publisher except in the case of brief quotations embodied in critical articles and reviews.

The materials available in this book are for informational purposes only and not for the purpose of providing legal, tax, or investment advice. US and foreign citizens considering utilization of the investment or immigration programs or strategies contained herein should consult with experienced legal, tax, and investment professionals as appropriate.

iUniverse books may be ordered through booksellers or by contacting:
iUniverse
1663 Liberty Drive
Bloomington, IN 47403
www.iuniverse.com
1-800-Authors (1-800-288-4677)

Because of the dynamic nature of the Internet, any web addresses or links contained in this book may have changed since publication and may no longer be valid. The views expressed in this work are solely those of the author and do not necessarily reflect the views of the publisher, and the publisher hereby disclaims any responsibility for them.

Any people depicted in stock imagery provided by Thinkstock are models, and such images are being used for illustrative purposes only. Certain stock imagery © Thinkstock.

Family photo, front and back cover: © Andres Rodriguez | Dreamstime.com

ISBN: 978-1-4759-8504-7 (sc)
ISBN: 978-1-4759-8503-0 (hc)
ISBN: 978-1-4759-8505-4 (e)

Library of Congress Control Number: 2013906537

Printed in the United States of America.

iUniverse rev. date: 4/23/2013

To learn more about investment-visa programs, visit:

FamilySecurityNow.com, icsinusa.com, or blog.icsinusa.com.

"Like" us on Facebook (ICSinUSA) and
"follow" us on Twitter (@ICSinUSA).

Brian Dickens can be reached at brian@icsinusa.com.

Contents

Preface ix

Acknowledgments. xiii

Introduction: Jorge's Story. xvii

Chapter 1	The Program:What Is EB-5 Immigrant Investment?	1
Chapter 2	The Details:What Are the Requirements for This Program?.	11
Chapter 3	Investing in the United States:Why the United States? Why Now?.	23
Chapter 4	Qualifying EB-5 Investments:How Do We Choose an Opportunity?	37
Chapter 5	The EB-5 Process for Investors:How Do We Make This Happen?.	59
Chapter 6	USCIS: Who Decides If We Get a Visa and How Long Will it Take?	73
Chapter 7	Immigration and Taxation:Can We Still Run Our Business in Our Home Country?	81
Chapter 8	The Process for Companies: How Does a US Business Qualify to Attract EB-5 Investment?	87

Chapter 9	Another US Investment-Visa Program: What if We Can't Quite Afford EB-5?	93
Chapter 10	A Shortage of Service Providers: How Do We Find Help If We Need It?	97
Chapter 11	Conclusions: What Do We Do First?	107

Appendices		111
Chapter A	EB-5 Checklists	113
Chapter B	I-526 Visa Petition Checklist	119
Chapter C	EB-5 Investment Case Studies	121
Chapter D	Trade and Investment Treaty Nations	129

Glossary of Terms 135

Bibliography 141

Endnotes 145

Preface

In November of 2011, I left Idaho state government, frustrated by an inability to effectively help Idaho companies and entrepreneurs find the investment capital they needed to succeed. I had just completed nearly four out of my six years at the Idaho Department of Commerce learning and working with the EB-5 Immigrant Investor Program—a permanent-resident-visa program administered by US Citizenship and Immigration Services (USCIS) that awards foreign citizens permanent US residency for investing at least US$500,000 in a US company and creating ten jobs for US workers. I was frustrated because there were investors worldwide who were interested in the EB-5 program, and there were companies and entrepreneurs in the United States who desperately needed their investment, and there were certainly US workers who needed the jobs, but government—at both the federal and state level—did a dismal job of matching the needs with the solutions.

Part of this was due to an inherent ineptitude that government appears to have relative to sales and marketing, coupled with a fickle political system that positions and repositions efforts and resources at a moment's notice based on political expediency, uneducated popular opinion of the day, and the momentary direction of the political wind. Another part of the problem was that as a government employee, my hands were tied when it came to directly promoting any specific investment opportunity and closing deals with investors. Also, working specifically for only one state—Idaho—there were a limited number of investment opportunities to promote, which made it more difficult to find investments to which foreign investors were attracted. I decided to start my own company and to try and manage better in the private sector processes that were being mismanaged in the public sector.

I founded Inversión Consultant Services in January of 2012. ICS is a full-service immigrant investment consulting firm specializing in assistance to foreign investors who hope to participate in US investment-visa programs and the entrepreneurs, companies, projects, and communities in the United States who wish to attract those investors.

As I worked to get my company going, I decided to focus my investor attraction efforts on Latin America and particularly Mexico. These markets did not hold the enormous capacity of eligible investors that China does, but they were much closer to home and less expensive to reach. Since I'd had some success attracting Mexican investors to investment-visa programs while in state government, I determined this was a good starting point.

While I remain committed to helping US companies attract investment to finance their efforts, along the way I developed an even greater commitment to helping foreign citizens who are struggling in unsafe, unstable, and oppressive situations in their current home countries. All over the world I have discovered families living in fear—unaware that a safer, more carefree and secure lifestyle is available to them.

The first step has been to educate the marketplace and raise awareness of investment-visa programs. I was not very surprised to learn how many people in Mexico (and most countries in fact) had never heard of immigrant investment programs. I quickly discovered that I was spending most of my time at investor attraction meetings and seminars explaining the basics of what the programs were and how they worked. I seldom encountered qualified investors who didn't need to go home after meeting me to do their own research and verify the legitimacy of the program before considering the specific US investment opportunities I had to show them. In spite of the cost, complexity, and time required to participate in US investment-visa programs, they still evoke a "too good to be true" reaction from most foreign citizens that must be overcome.

I wrote this book—which I hope spreads widely throughout foreign markets—for the purpose of multiplying my education efforts to some extent, and to improve the learning curve of interested investors. As a cautious investor myself and a licensed investment adviser, I understand the care that must be taken to understand the details of an investment opportunity. When the complexity of a visa program and the safety and security of an investor's family are added to the mix, understanding and confidence must be increased all the more.

Though I was born and raised in the United States, I struggled through the immigration process for my own family. As a young US Marine serving in the Far East, I met and married a young woman from the Philippines. I naïvely believed that bringing her to the United States would be a simple process. I wasn't prepared for the mountain of red tape and the intimidating bureaucratic process that followed, nor for the onerous and protracted, multi-decade process of bringing my new wife's family to the United States. I also did not have the resources to afford an expensive immigration attorney on either side of the Pacific Ocean. I had to wade through the sea of paperwork, investigations, and interviews by myself—often at odds with my military commanders, who were sure I was making a stupid decision marrying this girl. I was a US citizen, and I found the process daunting; I can only imagine the challenges I would have faced as a foreign citizen who barely spoke English! My family's experience gave me an understanding of the fear, uncertainty, and intimidation that the immigration process presents.

This book allows interested investors to thoroughly educate themselves about appropriate visa programs before they begin the journey of investigating specific investment opportunities and the various service providers in the marketplace waiting to assist them.

Acknowledgments

The people I have helped and those I may help in the future all owe their thanks to my wife, Christine, and our four beautiful children—Stephen, Olivia, Reagan, and Mia—who are so precious to me that the thought of harm coming to any of them motivates me to prevent harm coming to anyone else's family. I owe my family my life as well, because they have quite literally saved it.

I thank Jesus Christ, the origin and foundation of the United States of America, who blessed me with the supreme privilege of being born here. I thank our founding fathers and all who have given their lives to establish, defend, and protect the USA—preserving the land of the free and the home of the brave and the American Dream for all who care to strive for it.

I would like to acknowledge the following leaders in the investment-visa industry who have taught me and helped me along the way, who continue to guide me, and who have been good friends:

Raymond Ku, a widely respected pioneer of the Asian, Canadian, and US immigrant investment industry responsible for hundreds of millions of dollars of Chinese and Taiwanese immigrant investment over the past twenty-five years. Contrary to his protectionist and largely paranoid business philosophy, Raymond let me have a long glimpse inside his company and his circle of influence. My experience with him has shaped a great deal of my understanding of the immigrant investment industry and particularly the Asian market, for which I will always be grateful. In any business, it's always good to know the markets to avoid!

Stephen Yale-Loehr—in many people's opinion, and certainly mine, one of the brain trusts of the immigrant investment industry. Mr. Yale-Loehr is an esteemed professor at Cornell University and busy managing the immigrant investment segment of a top immigration law firm, Miller-Mayer, which he cofounded in Ithaca, New York. Yet he has never been too busy to answer the phone or to make a recommendation when I call to review a document.

Thanks also to Mr. Sima Muroff, who graciously allowed me to tag along on the development and marketing campaigns of his Idaho State Regional Center and to learn so much about the international marketing of an investment-visa opportunity.

And leaders in other industries who have impacted my life, my skills, and my ability to perform investment-visa work:

Donald Dietrich, former director of the Idaho Department of Commerce. Mr. Dietrich is one of the best bosses with whom I have had the pleasure of working. He had the vision for Idaho to capitalize on the investment and job-creation benefits of the immigrant investment program and the courage to implement his vision—rare in state government. I could not have gained the knowledge I needed to help the people I help without Don's commitment and support.

Brad Wiskerchen, Joel Bauer, and Eben Pagan, for giving me exposure to strategies and tactics for getting this program in front of as many people as possible—quite probably saving thousands more lives than I ever could have done alone. Without their encouragement, this book would probably never have been written.

Armando Orellana and Erika Leon at the Idaho-Mexico Trade Office, who worked tirelessly to help a fledgling black-sheep Idaho company get off the ground.

Dr. Kent Neupert at Boise State University, whose instruction and mentorship during my MBA experience, and leadership and encouragement relative to international business-plan competitions, guided me to the production of world-class business plans and inspired me to launch my own businesses.

Dr. Kevin Learned at the Idaho Small Business Development Center, who graciously exposed me to his grounded systems and processes for evaluating businesses and investment opportunities and who simultaneously prepared me for the capital-investment attraction process. In spite of his personal skepticism about the EB-5 program, Kevin was always generous with his time and excellent advice.

Finally, to my good friends Jorge and Olivia and their wonderful family. Jorge and Olivia have an indomitable spirit and tremendous patience. They have been faithful friends even when things haven't gone perfectly and have taught me a lot more about these systems and processes than I have taught them. Jorge has exemplified courage and fatherly responsibility and leadership in the face of terrible circumstances. Thanks for becoming my good friends!

INTRODUCTION
Jorge's Story

If any of my children was harmed in any way—but especially if one was killed—I would be devastated. It is one of the greatest fears of my life that something might happen to my wife or to one of our children. I believe it when people say that the worst tragedy that can befall a parent is to outlive a child. I watched the loss of my uncle, and subsequently my father, absolutely destroy my grandmother both mentally and physically. I've met mothers and fathers who have lost a child, and I believe them when they tell me that you never get over the anguish.

But what if I lost all of my children—either sequentially or simultaneously—through some catastrophe? I just can't even think about it … it shakes me to my core. Even more devastating than that, what if I lost a child or all of my children, and it was completely my fault and I could have prevented it? How would I ever recover from that? Would I take my own life? Would I completely lose my mind?

Jorge did not want to find out.

A successful tool and machinery importer, and a factory-owner in Durango, Mexico, Jorge lived comfortably with his family of five in an upscale but modest neighborhood. His boys grew up excelling in academics and athletics. They also grew up with the boys from next door, sons of another successful Mexican businessman, a good friend of Jorge's. They lived a comfortable and apparently ideal life in the kind of neighborhood where families look out for one another.

The city of Durango is in the heart of the central forest region of Mexico and is the center of the country's lumber, wood-products, and paper-products manufacturing industries. It is a picturesque setting with a charming blend of old-world Mexico, open wilderness, and modern commerce and industry. Unfortunately, it is also one of the centers of Mexico's marijuana industry and a stronghold of particularly violent drug criminals. The rugged, mountainous terrain and dense forests create an opportunity for marijuana growers and traffickers to conceal their wares and their activities.

Over the years, as drug-related criminal activity and violence became a bigger and bigger problem in Durango, Jorge taught his sons not to get mixed up with drugs, and to stay away from the people who were. His attitude was always that "we won't bother them, and they won't bother us." Live and let live, so to speak.

While stories of kidnapping and extortion started to spread throughout Mexico and the state of Durango, and the local and national media began to exploit the gory headlines, Jorge and his family thought of these as random and isolated events. They had occasional brushes with crime—theft, robbery—but nothing that would discourage them from going to school, participating in sports, going out for dinner and a movie, or running the family business right there in their home. They were happy.

One day in 2009, some thugs from one of the local drug cartels showed up at the next-door neighbors' house and demanded money, saying that if the father didn't pay, they would kill his sons—now young adult men. The father told them that he wasn't going to pay them anything and that they should get off his property. The next day, they came back and shot his sons dead in front of the entire neighborhood.

These were the boys who grew up with Jorge's sons. They played together, walked to school together, went to each other's birthday parties, swam together, ate together, camped, had sleepovers—everything young friends would do. They were good boys. Jorge loved them almost like his own sons. Now Jorge had to help his friend and neighbor bury those boys, and he watched his friend suffer the devastation of losing his sons. Jorge knew in his heart that he had been naïve—that it was only a matter of time before his family would be targeted and they would come for his sons. Relocation within Mexico did not seem to be a reasonable alternative, because similar tragic events were playing out in virtually every region in the country.

The next week, Jorge and his wife deposited the boys at their grandparents' house, loaded up the car, and used tourist visas to drive to the United States. They had heard about programs through which they could gain permanent US residency, and now they were investigating.

I had only been studying the EB-5 Immigrant Investor Program for about two years when Jorge and his wife showed up in Idaho. EB-5 awards permanent US residency to foreign citizens who invest at least US$500,000 in a US company and create ten jobs for US workers. I had worked with Idaho's trade office in Mexico to put together a small delegation of potential EB-5 investors to visit Idaho companies, and that same week, Jorge made contact with our trade office. Jorge toured Idaho with the group of investors for three days and made a decision to work with me. He had an uneasy sense of urgency that I didn't understand at the time. It was more than a year before he could tell me his story without breaking down in tears.

I worked to help Jorge get his family and his business moved to

Idaho and to match him with various service providers that could assist his family with any details I didn't feel comfortable handling (such as document translation, legal work, accounting, real estate, and building contracting). My job at the Idaho Department of Commerce placed limits on how closely I could get involved in Jorge's business, but I stayed as close as I could to learn the details of the EB-5 process. Through that process, Jorge's family and my family became friends.

Jorge's immigration attorney determined that because his three sons were all over twenty-one years of age—and in spite of the fact that his total investment in the United States would exceed US$1 million—it would be best for Jorge and his wife to enter the United States on the E-2 Treaty Investor visa. The E-2 visa is a temporary, renewable visa for investors and their employees that doesn't require as high an investment. Jorge could "upgrade" his and his wife's visas to EB-5 at a later date. This would allow their oldest son—the chief operations officer of their factory—to enter the United States as an E-2 employee. The two younger sons could simultaneously qualify for student visas by enrolling at Idaho colleges.

Jorge and his wife returned to Mexico, said good-bye to friends and family, and moved their entire business and three sons to Idaho with tourism visas. For various reasons, I do not recommend following this course of action—either with the visa process or with moving to the United States before residency status has been granted—but in Jorge's family's case, the reality of the criminal situation in Durango pushed them to act more hastily than they might have under different circumstances. This created a number of headaches and stumbling blocks in the process, as two of Jorge's sons had to work on obtaining their student visas under the deadline of impending tourist-visa and entry-permit expiration, and everyone involved had to make subsequent trips to Mexico for consular interviews. On the other hand, they were all safe and secure and legally in the United States. We would work out the details later. In the end, Jorge and his wife were granted status as E-2 investors, which they intend to change to EB-5 later by virtue of their qualifying investment. Two of their sons entered graduate programs at a state university, one of whom graduated with his master's degree and recently began his doctoral program in electrical engineering. Their oldest son is still seeking E-2 status, but ultimately decided to return to Mexico—where his own daughter still lives—while they wait for his approval.

Families in Mexico lose loved ones to abduction and extortion-driven murder every single day. El Consejo para la Ley y los Derechos Humanos (CLDH)—the Council for the Law and Human Rights in Mexico—recently published the statistic that 17,889 reported cases of kidnapping occurred in 2011. But they also mentioned that only one out of ten kidnappings gets reported.[1] That means that close to 180,000 abductions occurred last year—more than 490 per day!

Yet individuals and families all over Mexico prefer to ignore these statistics and the evening news—although they may take some personal security measures—and simply hope that tragedy never strikes them or their family.

Jorge determined that next door was close enough. He was pushed to make a life-changing decision for the sake of his family's safety. The change that he was proposing for himself and his family was frightening. He and his sons spoke only limited English, and his wife spoke none at all. Although he had significant international business and sales experience, he knew virtually nothing about starting or running a business in the United States. He didn't know where they would live, or how everything would turn out. However, the very real prospect of losing one of his family members was far more frightening than the prospect of starting a new life in the United States.

Scenarios like this play out all over the world. Perhaps in some countries, criminal violence is not a present threat, but there may be other strong motivations to seek refuge in the United States. Wealthy citizens in some countries have become targets for inflated taxes, nationalization of their assets, or other forms of government oppression. In some countries, people still face religious persecution. In still other countries, there may be limited education or employment opportunities for young adult children. Wherever a strong motivation exists to expatriate, US investment-visa programs represent a portal to the safe haven that wealthy foreign citizens seek.

This book is offered as a resource for those who wish to learn about these valuable programs, overcome fear of change, and lead their families to safety and security in the USA.

Jorge elected to move his existing business—in its entirety—to the United States, which makes his an excellent case study in relocation and expansion. Appendix C contains three alternative scenarios for EB-5 investment. Once you are familiar with the way the program works, refer to the hypothetical case studies as examples of how investment-visa programs might work for you and your family.

Thousands of middle-class and wealthy families are finding safe havens in the United States through various investment-visa programs. These families from all over the world are fleeing economic, political, and criminal instability in their home countries. They have lost faith in their government's ability to protect them, and in some cases the protection that they counted on has already failed them. In the worst of all situations, government and law-enforcement officials who are sworn to serve and protect citizens have become corrupted to the point of extorting them—

or worse, of serving, protecting and even abetting the criminals who target the wealthy.

No, participating in these programs is not without risk, and there is bound to be a significant emotional toll in uprooting yourself and your family from loved ones and from a place you have lived and breathed as your home for your entire life. But the risks and the costs that you must pay seem to me to be vastly overshadowed by the risks—in many places—of staying where you are and perhaps living in denial of the dangers.

Poor or unstable economic conditions are initially less threatening to wealthy citizenry from a physical standpoint; however, families rightfully fear the complete erosion of their savings and net worth as governments scramble to ward off economic and political collapse by imposing exorbitant, runaway taxation on the few who have any remaining money. Typically—as we have seen in Greece—economic instability melts down into violence and criminal activity, and the wealthy are soon targeted from multiple directions.

Economic instability and the resultant tax rape of the citizens in one country can spill over into adjacent, more stable countries, as we have seen in Europe, where German citizens likely face the enormous tax burden of bailing out half a dozen or more failed countries in the European Union, including Greece, Spain, Portugal, Italy, and others that may follow.

Economic and criminal instability can certainly precipitate political instability, and in countries like China, Vietnam, Iran, Russia, Egypt, and Venezuela—where a strong military is always a looming threat to its own citizens—the wealthy often seek to flee the potential nationalization of their assets.

There can also be—and have always been—positive motivations for a move to the United States, such as educational opportunities for children, employment or business opportunities, religious freedom, or a love interest. Increasingly, however, immigrants and nonimmigrants are seeking refuge from dangerous conditions in their home country, both physical and financial.

The United States continues to be a land of opportunity, with low crime rates, little governmental corruption, comparatively low marginal tax rates, and a high standard of living—all of this in spite of our own recent economic contraction. For citizens of many countries, the strength of their currency relative to the dollar, coupled with increased supplies and decreasing prices in the United States, has created a tremendous investment and buying opportunity. Many attractive communities in the United States offer a surprisingly low cost of living for people who may have become accustomed to a luxurious (and expensive) lifestyle in their home countries.

Investment-visa programs administered by US Citizenship and Immigration Services remain a little-known but effective vehicle for wealthy investors in foreign countries to gain access to accelerated permanent US residency and citizenship.

This book is intended as an educational introduction to US investment-visa programs and as a guide to citizens of foreign countries who may be eligible to participate in them. The book should never be construed as a suggestion that someone else's country is bad, or that the United States is better. If you love your country as I love mine, and you are happy and secure there, then by all means, you and your family should stay. Or if you are determined, no matter how difficult conditions in your country have become, to stay there and do whatever it takes to improve those conditions—to fight against crime syndicates, or government waste or corruption, or tyranny—then I admire and respect you for your conviction. I would probably feel the same way.

My experience, however—or I should say, the experience of my newfound friends, which I have observed—has been that while governments and armies may someday be able to overcome drug syndicates and internal corruption and economic collapse to restore stability and security, the unarmed civilian population will be the unfortunate victims (and the bankroll) in a war that they could never have won. And perhaps worst of all, the innocent children of the wealthy are going to pay much too high a price, often their very lives.

My heart is to help the people I *can* help—and particularly their children—to find and enjoy the kind of safety and security that my family and I experience at home in the United States. I have said many times in seminars and meetings with interested foreign investors that I wish it was in my power to bring safety and security to people in the homes and countries where they live now. I know what "home" means and how much it means to people all over the world. Alas, I don't possess such power. What I believe I have found, however, is a means to lead people to safety and security in *my* home—the United States. I hope to increase safety and security for these people and their families as many times as possible.

I've been asked a few times, "Does it feel right to just help the rich people?" Well, no, not entirely, but two things help me to rationalize my efforts in this regard: (1) the wealthy are being disproportionately targeted, and in many cases ruthlessly and repeatedly victimized, and (2) the upper middle class and wealthy are the ones qualified for the programs I have studied. I will help others when I can, but I have to help those I am able to right now. Eventually, through the generation of some service income, I hope to provide an increasing amount of immigration assistance to less affluent foreign citizens as well.

For those readers of my book who are looking for a safe haven—a refuge from the uncertainty and instability they may be experiencing where they live—I hope this book will be an assurance that there is a safe and secure alternative, and an encouragement to come and get it.

I don't want the title of my book to be misleading. There is a popular saying in the United States, often attributed to Benjamin Franklin, that the only things certain in life are death and taxes. I know that people who live in the United States face dangers, insecurity, and economic instability from time to time. But comparatively speaking, these situations are far more isolated and infrequent than in many countries around the world. Therefore, the relative certainty of experiencing sustained security, stability, and tranquility for people living in the United States is higher.

The programs that my book describes require a significant monetary commitment. The required investment coupled with the associated administrative fees put US investment-visa programs out of the reach of probably 95 percent or more of the world's population. What readers will learn from these pages, however, is that the main price of admission to these programs—the investment—may not only be returned to the investor, but possibly even with a capital gain. Ultimately, through referral incentives and other mechanisms, investors may even recover some or all of their administrative fees and other out-of-pocket costs.

Through careful selection of an investment opportunity, and careful selection of service providers to assist them, investors stand a reasonable likelihood of actually being *paid* to remove their families from danger, to embrace a tranquil existence, and to obtain financial stability.

In the first two chapters of *Certain Security*, I will describe the history and detailed requirements of the EB-5 Immigrant Investor Program. In chapter 3, I'll explain why this may be the best time in history to invest and live in the United States. In chapter 4, we'll take a look at choosing a qualified EB-5 investment.

In chapter 5, I'll introduce my proven four-step process

for successfully navigating US investment-visa programs, and in chapter 6 we'll examine US Citizenship and Immigration Services and its process for administering your visa. Chapter 7 presents general information relative to taxation and immigrant investment. Chapter 8 explains how US companies become eligible to attract these investments.

In chapter 9, I'll provide some detailed information about one other investment-visa program, and in chapter 10, I'll share some secrets to identifying qualified service providers to help investors through the investment-visa process. Finally, in chapter 11, we'll wrap up with some conclusions, encouragement to move forward, and an outline of your next steps.

CHAPTER 1

The Program: What Is EB-5 Immigrant Investment?

US investment-visa programs have been around for a long time. Even the EB-5 program is more than twenty years old, and yet these programs have existed in relative obscurity in the United States until only recently. On a global basis, there is even less awareness. In this first chapter, we'll take a look at the beginnings of the EB-5 program, see how it has grown, and check in on some of the program's recent developments.

Early History

The US Congress established the EB-5 (Employment-Based, Fifth Preference) Immigrant Investor Program in 1990. It is widely believed that the program came about as a result of Canada's success at attracting Hong Kongers—fearful of Chinese Central Government oppression, persecution, and nationalization of assets—when Hong Kong reverted to Chinese control in 1999. While Congress had previously attempted to create immigrant investment programs, the Immigration Act of 1990 was the bill that successfully passed both houses of Congress and earned President George H. W. Bush's signature into law.

The mass exodus from Hong Kong—primarily to major

cities like Vancouver and Toronto—created a massive economic boom in those cities and throughout Canada. The expatriated Hong Kongers brought more than just the CN$250,000 required for their visas. They brought the rest of their economy as well. Skyscrapers, luxury homes, and all of the infrastructure needed to support such growth went up seemingly overnight. American leadership felt that the United States should do something to participate in attracting these wealthy investors too.

So in the Immigration Act of 1990, Congress devised a program that would be administered by the Immigration and Naturalization Service—the predecessor of today's US Citizenship and Immigration Services (USCIS)—which would permit a foreign citizen from any country to invest a minimum of US$1 million in a US business, leave that investment fully at risk for at least two years, and create ten permanent full-time jobs for authorized US workers in exchange for permanent resident visas for the investor and the investor's immediate family. Ten thousand visas were set aside each year for the program. The Immigration Act also included a provision to permit a lower investment threshold—US$500,000—in rural areas or preidentified areas with high unemployment called Targeted Employment Areas or TEAs, and three thousand visas were set aside for those investments.[2] The EB-5 Immigrant Investor Program was born.

In 1993, Congress further modified the program by establishing the EB-5 Immigrant Investment Regional Center Pilot Program—which enabled the pooling of many EB-5 investments in regional centers for much larger development projects. Regional centers have the dual benefit of preapproved projects and easier satisfaction of job-creation requirements through the ability to count direct, indirect, and induced job creation using preliminary economic analysis. Congress allocated three thousand visas to investments through regional centers annually.

The EB-5 programs experienced fits and starts in the early years for several reasons. Typically poor marketing and publicity by the US government, along with less-expensive and less-regulated programs in other countries, seemed to limit the US programs' attractiveness. The regional center pilot program even experienced a brief suspension in the late '90s. Still, several million dollars of investment were attracted to early regional centers in Seattle and Los Angeles from Hong Kong, Taiwan, South Korea, and Japan.

The pivotal shot in the arm for the EB-5 program came in 2003 when—to everyone's amazement—the Chinese Central Government announced that it had no objection to its citizens participating in investment-visa and other immigration programs. This announcement sent a wave of enthusiasm and growth through immigrant investment programs all around the globe, but particularly the EB-5 program. China and the US immigrant investment program got up to speed and fully into alignment just in time for the US economic meltdown of 2008.

Rapid Growth

In late 2007, when I began to study the EB-5 program while working for the Idaho Department of Commerce, the USCIS website was only acknowledging the existence of nineteen regional centers nationwide. Of those, perhaps only twelve had been active in the marketplace and had attracted any investment, and only perhaps four of those could be considered truly "successful"—attracting US$10 million or more. During 2008 and 2009, when I was preparing Idaho's first regional-center application and consulting/advising on three additional efforts, the number of approved regional centers swelled to between sixty and ninety. As the US real-estate bubble burst in 2008, many real-estate developers—desperate to recover after losing their shirts in the crash, and unable to get debt financing from the shell-shocked banking industry—discovered EB-5 and glommed onto it like a life preserver in the middle of an oceanic storm. Many recognized the program as an inexpensive and fast process to raise investment capital and save their foundering projects, so they rushed to establish regional centers and gain USCIS approval.

Then, for the beginning of the first federal fiscal quarter of 2010 (October), USCIS imposed a US$6,230 processing fee for EB-5 regional-center applications for the first time. Previously there had been no charge to submit and adjudicate an application. The result was a massive backlog of applications at USCIS, and a 300 to 400 percent increase in the number of regional centers, as the desperation of the real-estate and investment industries combined with a mad dash to beat the September 30 deadline for a "free" regional-center application.

At the time of this writing, the USCIS website acknowledges 243 approved EB-5 regional centers; however, several of those are no longer active.[3] Table 1-1 reflects USCIS's most recent regional-center figures as presented at a 2012 quarterly stakeholder meeting in October. This would seem to indicate that more than thirty regional centers have lost their approved status over the life of the program.

Visits to the websites of active regional centers reveal that they are responsible for a broad variety of industries and projects, ranging from alternative energy to motion pictures, from equity investment funds to ski resorts, from basketball arenas and convention centers to gold mines. The vast majority, however—regardless of their target industry—are some variation on residential or commercial real-estate projects.

Table 1-1: Approved EB-5 Regional Centers by Year

U.S. Citizenship and Immigration Services (USCIS) Number of Approved EB-5 Regional Centers Fiscal Years 2007-2012	
FY 2007	11
FY 2008	25
FY 2009	72
FY 2010	114
FY 2011	174
FY 2012	209

Source: US Citizenship and Immigration Services[4]

I would conservatively estimate that the percentage of truly active and truly "successful" regional centers relative to the total number approved has actually declined by half since 2007. In other words, if twelve out of nineteen (63 percent) were active in 2007 and four out of nineteen (21 percent) were successful, I would estimate that no more than 30 percent are active today (69 out of 230) with 10 percent (23) successful, having attracted more than US$10 million. The actual numbers could be significantly lower. I would attribute the deflated numbers to a strong consolidation of the industry as a few regional-center players have perfected their offerings, their marketing plans, and their processes and have emerged as "investments of choice" in the major Chinese marketplace—making it hard for new players to gain entry. I would also suggest that many of the more recently approved applicants entered the industry without a clue as to what work and investment would actually be required to successfully attract investment to a regional center. Regional centers without a significant bankroll and without a lot of intestinal fortitude usually fold their tent pretty quickly.

With respect to participation by immigrant investors, the EB-5 program remains underutilized. As Table 1-2 reflects, the

United States has never approached the ten thousand visas per year allotted to the EB-5 program.

Table 1-2: Annual EB-5 Visa Usage

U.S. Citizenship and Immigration Services (USCIS) EB-5 Visa Usage Fiscal Years 2005-2012	
Fiscal Year	Total EB-5 Visas Issued
FY 2012 (YTD)*	2,364
FY 2011	3,463
FY 2010	1,885
FY 2009	4,218
FY 2008	1,360
FY 2007	806
FY 2006	744
FY 2005	158
*Estimate of 2012 visas issued YTD reported by the Dept. of State as of 01/17/2012.	

Source: US Citizenship and Immigration Services[5]

Additionally, USCIS has suggested in public meetings and via memoranda that the ten thousand visas is not a hard quota—that more visas could be allotted to EB-5 annually if they were needed.

Recent Developments

In addition to the continued swelling and contracting of the EB-5 regional-center market, the following sections highlight other recent developments in the industry.

The US$1 Million Threshold

While I would not necessarily call this a *recent* development, its impact on the EB-5 industry continues to evolve. The provision of US$500,000 EB-5 investments for rural areas and TEAs has rendered US$1 million EB-5 opportunities virtually uncompetitive. Conventional wisdom would suggest that a superior US$1 million investment opportunity should be able to attract investors over a marginal US$500,000 opportunity. It also stands to reason that some of the best business and investment opportunities are going to be in low-unemployment Metropolitan Statistical Areas (MSAs) that are ineligible for the US$500,000 threshold.

In the most mature EB-5 markets, brokers and agents have groomed EB-5 investors to believe that their greatest return on investment (ROI) is the US visa, and therefore to expect low monetary ROIs. As a result, investors are not being attracted by superior investment opportunities in cities with strong economies where the US$500,000 investment is not available. Foreign investors recognize that they derive the same benefits for half of the investment when they invest in a project with rural or TEA status, so they seek out and prefer those opportunities.

Ultimately, it would be better for the US economy if the US$1 million threshold were eliminated, because many more jobs would be created and low-to-average unemployment areas would not be effectively exempted from the program.

The unintended consequence of what was thought to be an incentive to invest in distressed areas has been the wholesale elimination of EB-5 investment in economically strong urban areas. To counter this trend, some states have looked for ways to exercise their TEA designation authority and to increase the number of TEAs where EB-5 projects can locate *within* some of their MSAs. When localized high unemployment exists in a subregion (census tract) of an MSA, states can succeed with this strategy. Some states, however, will not be able to accomplish this when an MSA's unemployment is more uniform, and these MSAs will remain ineligible for the US$500,000 immigrant investment.

Simultaneously, some urban areas that have experienced extensive out-migration and have become distressed, depressed, or even blighted may remain unattractive for EB-5 investment because their unemployment rate does not qualify for TEA status while more affluent areas do qualify, largely through happenstance. These anomalies can and should be addressed through new legislation or rule-making.

US$1 million EB-5 investments do continue to occur occasionally, but they are made almost exclusively through direct EB-5 investments, where investors have a clear idea of the type of business in which they want to invest and where they maintain tighter managerial control of the investment.

A Permanent EB-5 Program

EB-5 is a permanent program, codified in federal regulations (8 CFR 204.6) since 1991, setting aside ten thousand permanent resident visas per year for immigrant investors. Since its inception in 1993, the EB-5 Immigrant Investment Regional Center Pilot Program has been renewed repeatedly—for between one and three years—frequently through Congress's continuing resolution process. In 2012, the House and Senate voted to extend the program through September 30, 2015, and took a small step toward making the program permanent by omitting the word "pilot" from the reauthorization bill's language. Three bills—S-3245, S-642, and H.R.-2972—have been drafted in recent years to permanently reauthorize the program so that the periodic renewals would not be necessary. Although the program has been renewed each time it has "sunset," each sunset seems to send ripples of uncertainty through the industry and the investor marketplace, and a permanent reauthorization would eliminate this periodic instability.[6]

Occupant Tenant Employment

Regional centers, and even some direct EB-5 investment projects (those not made through a regional center), have faced some scrutiny and challenges from USCIS in 2011 and 2012 pertaining to their employment creation. USCIS has taken the position that jobs created by the occupant-tenants of a development project—as opposed to the *owners* of the project—should not count toward direct employment numbers of the project, and hence should not have employment multipliers applied to them. USCIS prefers to treat occupant-tenant employees as indirect or induced employees. This has severely diminished the overall employment numbers of businesses and projects in some cases and consequently has reduced the number of EB-5 investors that a given project can accommodate. These challenges present a problem for project developers who intend to count the direct employment by businesses that move into the facilities they have built with EB-5 investment dollars.

As an example, a developer who builds, owns, and operates a hotel on a given property would get credit for all of the full-time employees that he proposes to hire, and then an industry jobs multiplier would be used to determine how many indirect and induced jobs those original *direct* jobs would precipitate. USCIS would give the project credit for the sum total of all of those jobs. Conversely, if a developer builds a hotel for a hotel chain that leases the building and subsequently hires its staff, USCIS has indicated that it will treat those jobs as indirect jobs of the project, and as such, no multipliers would be applied to them in the economic impact analysis. The jobs created by the occupant-tenant hotel chain would not count as direct employment of the project.

While it would seem that USCIS should be pleased with any and all permanent full-time jobs that are facilitated by an EB-5 investment—particularly through a regional center—they have recently expressed a refusal to consider this direct employment unless the original developers of the project actually own the company occupying the facility and hire the workers. This stance seems counterintuitive to a job-creation program, since jobs created by a tenant must certainly be *indirect* jobs created in the value chain (downstream) of the project developer/owner.[7]

Development of New Markets

While China remains the single largest source of EB-5 investors in US projects, understanding and utilization of the program continues to expand into new markets throughout the world. Essentially, wherever there is some strong motivation to expatriate, the EB-5 and other investment-visa opportunities are attractive. Violent crime, government oppression, runaway taxation, economic or political instability, and limited education or employment opportunities all portend a demand for investment-visa programs. Mexico, Central America, South America, Ireland, Spain, Greece, Germany, Egypt, Iran, and Russia have all seen increased interest in US investment-visa programs in recent months and years.

Now that we have some familiarity with the history of EB-5, in chapter 2 we'll dig into the details of the program.

CHAPTER 2

The Details: What Are the Requirements for This Program?

In this chapter, we will examine the detailed requirements of the EB-5 Immigrant Investor Program and its qualification criteria.

Investor Qualifications

Accredited Investor

EB-5 investors must meet the US Securities and Exchange Commission (SEC) definition of an "accredited investor." Accredited investors are deemed to have the education and experience to understand and assume the risk of a given investment and the capacity to absorb any potential loss as a result of that investment. The SEC defines an accredited investor as having at least US$1 million in net worth—excluding the primary home—*or* an average of either $200,000 per year in individual annual income or $300,000 in household annual income for each of the preceding two years, and an expectation of the same income level in the current year. While I have not seen USCIS apply strict scrutiny to the accredited status of all EB-5 investors, potential investors should provide evidence that they fit some of the criteria listed above.

Clean Money

EB-5 investors must show documentary evidence to prove that their investment funds were derived from legitimate sources. The US Department of Homeland Security, USCIS, and the US State Department work to insure that no monies derived from the drug trade, money laundering, terrorism, or any other illegal activity are invested through investment-visa programs and/or used to grant access to the United States to foreign criminals.

Legitimate sources of EB-5 investment funds include:

- Earnings from petitioner's business
- Gifts
- Sales transactions
- Stocks
- Retirement funds
- Loans secured by petitioner's assets
- Inheritance
- Real estate
- Sale of petitioner's business assets
- General wealth accumulation[8]

Typically, up to five years of personal and business bank statements, tax returns, pay stubs, and other financial documents are used to satisfy these requirements.

Good Citizenship

EB-5 investors and their immediate family members must pass the same background investigations typically required for any US visa. Foreign citizens with military service, criminal arrest records, or associations with subversive organizations or individuals will face tougher scrutiny as their visa applications are adjudicated. Probably most importantly, truthful attestations and representations must be made on applications and in interviews at all times. The discovery—by any US official—that a lie has been told or that evidence has been fabricated will almost certainly result in immediate denial of a visa petition.

EB-5 applicants and their families must submit copies of many identifying documents, including birth and marriage certificates, passports, any existing visas, and school and university graduation certificates. An applicant who intends to expand or relocate an existing foreign business must also submit several business documents to prove experience and success in the given business activity, such as business licenses, financial records, and property titles.

Any document originally produced in a foreign language must be accompanied by an English translation prepared by a certified translator.

Direct EB-5 Investments

In this section, I will describe the requirements of EB-5 investments made directly into commercial enterprises—distinct from regional-center investments.

Type of Business

A foreign citizen or a group of foreign citizens may make a qualifying EB-5 investment directly into a US business. The business may be an existing foreign business of his or her own that the investor relocates or expands into the United States; it may be a new business of the investor's own concept that he or she launches in the United States; it may be a new partnership with US owners of a new or existing US business; or it may be an investment in the purchase or partnership of an existing, troubled US business.

Employment Creation

Ten permanent full-time jobs must be created for each EB-5 investor, and in the case of a direct investment project, all of the previously authorized US workers must be direct employees of the commercial enterprise receiving the investment. For example, for a project receiving US$1.5 million from three EB-5 investors, the company receiving the investment must hire thirty direct full-time employees within two and a half years of the anniversary of the investments. While investors and their family members may work for the company and draw reasonable salaries or wages, their employment may not count toward the total of ten employees per investor. "Permanent" jobs are defined as those expected to last at least two full years. "Full-time" jobs are defined as requiring thirty hours or more per week. No indirect or induced job creation counts toward the requirement.

Rural and Targeted Employment Areas

An investor may invest US$500,000 in a qualified business if the investment and the job creation will be realized in a rural area or a Targeted Employment Area (TEA). A rural area is defined as an area outside any Metropolitan Statistical Area (MSA) *and* outside the boundary of any community with a population of twenty thousand or more. A TEA is defined as any geographic or geopolitical region *within* an MSA or within the boundaries of a community with a population of twenty thousand or more that is experiencing unemployment of at least 150 percent of the US national average at the time of the investment. Otherwise, any investment made within an MSA or a community with twenty thousand or more people must be for a minimum of US$1 million.

As was mentioned briefly in chapter 1, the US$500,000 investment threshold has rendered projects—both direct and regional-center investments—with the US$1 million investment requirement virtually uncompetitive. In spite of how compelling or lucrative any given investment opportunity may be, educated investors quickly become aware of the fact that they can get all the same benefits of the EB-5 program while risking only 50 percent of the money. Even investors who may be willing to invest many more dollars in a project prefer not to tie up more than US$500,000 in the EB-5 process. For this reason, direct EB-5 investment companies, like regional centers, strive to locate their projects within rural areas or TEAs, or to have their current locations designated as TEAs if possible.

At-Risk Investment

EB-5 investors must leave their investment dollars fully at risk for a minimum of two years. This means that they may not withdraw or be repaid any of their invested principal in the form of dividends, distributions, or any other form of payment during the first two years of their investment. Importantly, the nature of a "fully" at-risk investment implies that investors may not be promised or guaranteed *any* reimbursement of their invested principal *at all*—not even more than two years in the future, *after* the at-risk period of their investment has passed.

A company or project may (and should) provide the investor with a repayment plan that lays out the timeline of projected reimbursement of principal, but no guarantee of such reimbursement may be either expressed or implied. In fact, the Private Placement Memorandum (PPM) or offering document that an investor typically signs to subscribe to an EB-5 project must clearly and boldly describe the nature of the project's risk and the potential for the investor to lose all of his or her investment. The offering documents—including subscription agreement, PPM, operating agreement, and partnership agreement—generally resemble documents from a Regulation D offering of exempt securities to accredited US investors (pursuant to Regulation D of the Securities Act of 1930). The investor bears 100 percent of the risk associated with his or her investment.

As mentioned previously, investors and/or their family members may be employed by the commercial enterprise and derive a reasonable wage for their work within the general operating expenses of the company, but such payments must be carefully documented so as not to be construed by USCIS as a withdrawal of invested principal.

Pooled Direct Investments

Two or more EB-5 investors may be pooled together for a qualified EB-5 investment in the same commercial enterprise. It should be remembered, however, that the direct employment creation requirement increases by ten for each investor. It becomes increasingly difficult to fund and sustain the employment of the necessary workers beyond a certain number of investors. For example: If a company attracts US$10 million in EB-5 investment from twenty foreign investors, it may be very difficult for that company (or any company for that matter) to hire and sustain the full-time employment of two hundred people over the course of the ensuing two and a half years—together with all other operational expenses—with only US$10 million. For this reason, companies and projects requiring more than US$5 million in EB-5 investment typically pursue the creation of an EB-5 regional center, or partnership with an existing regional center.

The Application

A direct EB-5 investor completes a single I-526 Immigrant Petition for Alien Entrepreneur for the entire immediate family. The application must include evidentiary documents that describe in detail the nature of the investment and the commercial enterprise receiving it. A detailed business plan and financial statements—tailored for the EB-5 program—along with any and all legal and offering documents must be submitted to USCIS with the I-526 petition. Here again, any document prepared in a foreign language must be accompanied by a certified translation. In the case of a direct EB-5 investment, USCIS evaluates both the investor and the commercial enterprise in the adjudication process.

Regional-Center Investments

EB-5 immigrant investment regional centers are preapproved by USCIS to market their projects to foreign investors and to utilize economic modeling to forecast total direct, indirect, and induced job creation that will result from a given investment. Regional centers are intended to pool the EB-5 investments of many foreign investors to fund larger development projects. To date, the largest known project has been a US$300 million convention-center project in Philadelphia, Pennsylvania, which attracted more than US$125 million in EB-5 investment. Regional centers, their projects, and the investments they attract have some unique characteristics that I will describe in this section.

Regional-Center Approval

An EB-5 regional center and each of its investment projects must gain advanced approval from USCIS before it can be approved. A hopeful regional center must submit a detailed I-924 Application for Regional Center Under the Immigrant Investor Pilot Program along with a US$6,230 filing fee to USCIS and endure an exhaustive four- to six-month review process. The application must include a detailed business plan for both the regional center and any prospective investment project along with an extensive economic analysis of the project prepared by a professional regional economist. The regional-center applicant must describe the geographic region that the regional center will serve, any rural areas or TEAs within that region, the marketing and operations plan for the regional center as well as for the prospective project, and detailed financial projections for both the center and the project.

The economic model must utilize recognized econometric methodology to forecast how many direct, indirect, and induced jobs will be created as a result of the proposed investment in the region and industries targeted by the regional center. Direct jobs are those that will be created by the project or commercial enterprise itself; indirect jobs are those that are projected to be created upstream and downstream from the commercial activity of the project (suppliers, distributors, etc.); and induced jobs are those projected to spring up as other vendors and peripheral businesses open and hire employees to serve the project company and its employees. Economists use accepted formulas and multipliers to first determine how many *direct* jobs will result from a given investment, and then to derive indirect and induced employment numbers from that resultant number of direct jobs.

Finally, the regional-center application must include drafts of all of the legal and investment offering documents that the regional center intends to provide to its prospective investors. To adjudicate and ultimately approve or reject the application, USCIS may require additional information through its Request for Evidence (RFE) process.

Investor Requirements

EB-5 regional-center investors have essentially the same qualifications as direct EB-5 investors, except that the regional-center project is preapproved, so that instead of sending business plans and a description of the commercial enterprise to USCIS for approval, a regional-center investor merely includes a copy of the regional center's USCIS approval letter. Investors in a regional-center project will frequently be subscribing to some sort of limited partnership with other EB-5 investors, so limited-partnership agreements, along with all other legal and offering documents, are included with the investor's I-526 Immigrant Petition by Alien Entrepreneur.

The Conditional Visa

Approved EB-5 investors—whether through direct investment or a regional center—and members of their immediate family are granted conditional permanent resident visas to the United States. USCIS alerts the US Department of State, and an interview is scheduled for the investor's family at the US consulate in their home country. At the consular interview, additional questions are asked, and if all goes well, the visa is provided to each family member. The conditional visa is awarded for a period of two years.

Removal of Conditions

Within ninety days of the expiration of the conditional visa, the EB-5 investor must submit to USCIS an I-829 Petition by Entrepreneur to Remove Conditions, which describes how the investment was used, that it remained at risk for the full two years, and that ten permanent full-time jobs were created as a result of the investment. In the case of direct EB-5 investment, the I-829 petition includes evidence of direct employment by the commercial enterprise. Usually, I-9 Employment Eligibility Verification forms for each active employee are used to satisfy this requirement. In the case of a regional-center investment, the I-829 shows proof that the proposed investment was indeed made in the industry and region that were targeted, and in the time frame that the project plan implied. If there have been no material changes from the original plan, then USCIS will accept that the requisite jobs have been created and approve the I-829. If, on the other hand, material changes to the business plan have occurred in the course of the project, the regional center and the investors may be required to show proof of at least the requisite direct employment, and that such employment occurred in the industries and communities as planned.

Once USCIS is satisfied that the investment remained at risk and that the requisite jobs have been created, the agency will approve the I-829 petition and award unconditional permanent resident visas to the entire immediate family.

Table 2-1 reflects the respective approval rates of I-526 and I-829 petitions by USCIS over the past eight years.

Table 2-1: EB-5 Approval Rates by Petition and Year

U.S. Citizenship and Immigration Services (USCIS) Immigrant Petition by Alien Entrepreneur (I-526) and Petition by Entrepreneur to Remove Conditions (I-829) Service-wide Receipts, Approvals, Denials Fiscal Years 2005-2012 (Third Quarter)								
	I-526 Petition				I-820 Petition			
Fiscal Year	Receipts	Approvals	Denials	Approval %	Receipts	Approvals	Denials	Approval %
2005	332	179	156	53%	37	184	112	62%
2006	486	336	124	73%	89	106	108	50%
2007	776	473	148	76%	194	111	49	69%
2008	1257	640	120	84%	390	159	68	70%
2009	1028	1262	207	86%	437	347	56	86%
2010	1955	1369	165	89%	768	274	56	83%
2011	3805	1563	371	81%	2345	1067	46	96%
2012	4156	3002	775	79%	546	639	42	94%
Grand Total	13795	8824	2066	81%	4806	2887	537	84%

Source: US Citizenship and Immigration Services[9]

The overwhelming majority of petitions are approved, although in 2012 the I-526 approval percentage decreased slightly—probably due to a large number of new and inexperienced regional centers and service providers.

This chapter has provided a detailed explanation of the EB-5 program and its requirements. In chapter 3, we'll consider the US investment and residency opportunity based on the 2013 global economy.

CHAPTER 3

Investing in the United States: Why the United States? Why Now?

The United States has not escaped the economic turmoil of the last five years—much of which it had a key role in precipitating. The unchecked indiscretion of Wall Street; what many perceive as a fiscal-policy failure of the US government; and the "irrational exuberance" surrounding the US residential and commercial real-estate industries in the mid-2000s combined to create one of the biggest economic collapses in US history.

US governmental leadership—particularly those agencies and offices pertaining to economics—compounded the resultant economic instability with an expensive overhaul and nationalization of the US health-care system and ill-advised, taxpayer-funded stimulus and corporate-bailout packages. These economic conditions will almost certainly result in increased marginal tax rates for virtually all US citizens, and it will be some time before markets, industries, and employment stabilize and recover to pre-2008 levels.

All of these difficulties notwithstanding, there may never have been a better time to invest in the United States, and the opportunities for living and working in the United States also remain excellent. This chapter will examine the conditions that make the United States an attractive alternative for living, working, and investing, and will encourage skeptical foreign investors to reconsider their position on such an investment. EB-5 and other investment-visa programs may provide a unique opportunity to flee difficult conditions abroad and to simultaneously benefit from approaching US economic expansion.

The "Why now?" portion of this chapter's title is really answered more appropriately by the economic and personal security condition of the foreign investor than any fluctuating economic activity in the United States or the rest of the world. If your family is in danger—either physical or financial—then "Why now?" has already been answered. Nevertheless, we will examine other US and global conditions that make the United States a great opportunity today.

Taxes

In spite of all the negative economic activity of the preceding five years, the United States remains among the world's least taxed societies from a marginal tax-rate perspective. While, as noted, the US tax rate is somewhat likely to increase to support economic recovery, it is doubtful that such increases will result in the United States falling behind many other countries' tax rates on a comparative basis—particularly since many of the other countries with attractive marginal tax rates are facing economic catastrophes of their own.

Member nations of the European Union (EU), for example, are faced with the stark reality of having to shore up the economies of their less responsible neighbor countries—a reality that will almost certainly be solved through hyper-taxation of the wealthy throughout Europe. The economically weaker European nations will follow Spain, Ireland, and Greece into bankruptcy as their national debts surpass their gross national product and their wealthy citizens move to tax havens abroad. Meanwhile, strong economies like Germany and France will bear the brunt of bailing out the entire EU. The wealthy in those countries will likely either face hyper-taxation or similarly relocate.

The US taxpayer will undoubtedly play some role in bolstering the economies of foreign countries, and our tax rates will reflect the initial climb out of our own economic distress, but the independence of the US dollar and its foundational support from natural resources and still-significant national wealth will insulate the United States from the tax-rate inflation that other countries in the world will face. Once US economic recovery is well-established, revenues from the breadth of the tax base will diminish our need for higher rates, and political pressure will likely be brought to bear to lower those rates.

Figure 3-1 illustrates the global tax comparison of a sample of countries based on total 2010 tax revenues as a percent of gross domestic product (GDP). It will be interesting to see where these rates shake out in the future and how our misery compares!

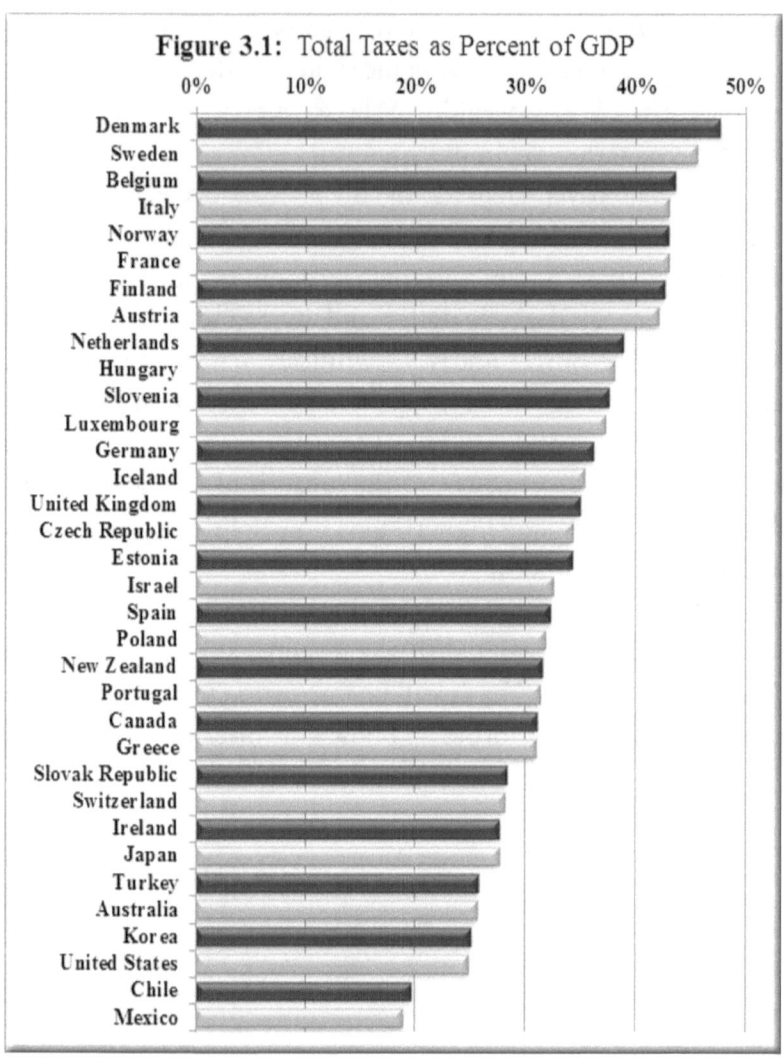

Data Source: Organisation for Economic Co-operation and Development[10]

Analysis of the best country based on this data—Mexico—is particularly interesting. Mexico has experienced unprecedented prosperity recently, which has attracted an unprecedented number of immigrants, both legal and illegal, from Central American countries. Simultaneously, the United States' economic woes have caused unemployed Mexican immigrants in the United States to repatriate back to Mexico. This inflow of people has created an enormous strain on public services that, together with increasing law-enforcement and national-defense costs, will almost certainly precipitate an increase in taxes.

The Value of the US Dollar

The United States' economic difficulties have created a significant shift in the value of many countries' currencies relative to the US dollar. This condition—coupled with the drastically reduced prices for some goods, services, and real property (which we will discuss next)—has created an opportunity in which foreign investors in these countries can benefit significantly.

Investors can exchange their foreign currencies for historically higher numbers of dollars, and then use those dollars to make purchases and investments in commodities and industries that are cheaper because of natural supply-and-demand forces. Figure 3.2 illustrates the trending value of some currencies relative to the US dollar.

The attractive US investment opportunity of a newly built, four-bedroom house in Texas that is currently selling for US$150,000.00 is even more attractive to a Mexican citizen who can buy more dollars with her pesos than ever before.

These global monetary conditions are likely to be short-lived, however—as we are already seeing signs (in late 2012) that the world's currency valuations relative to the US dollar are adjusting and stabilizing. On the other hand, a monetary decision by the Chinese Central Government to float its powerful currency may shake things up once again.

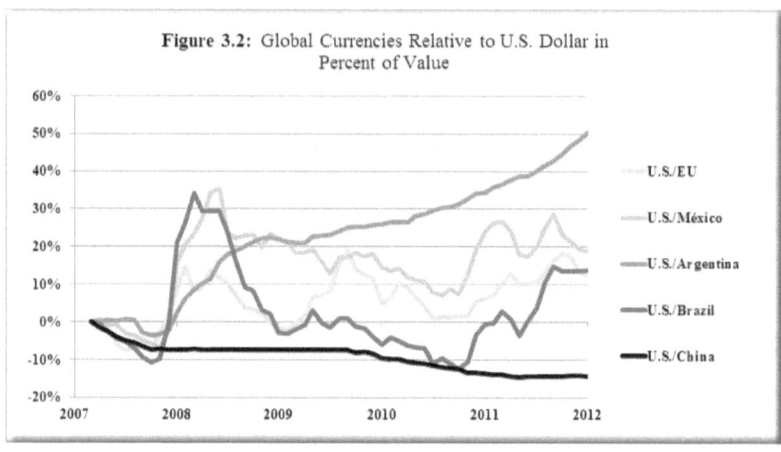

Data Source: OANDA[11]

Bottoming US Prices

Struggles and instability in the US economy create surplus supplies of goods and services throughout the country and eventual decreases in prices. Economic recovery will necessarily stimulate inflation of prices—perhaps even hyperinflation—but in the meantime, prices remain low because of surpluses. Prices on products that are strictly dependent on transportation fuels or high production energy costs have remained high in the United States. Figure 3.3 illustrates a continuing inflationary trend in the US consumer price index (CPI).

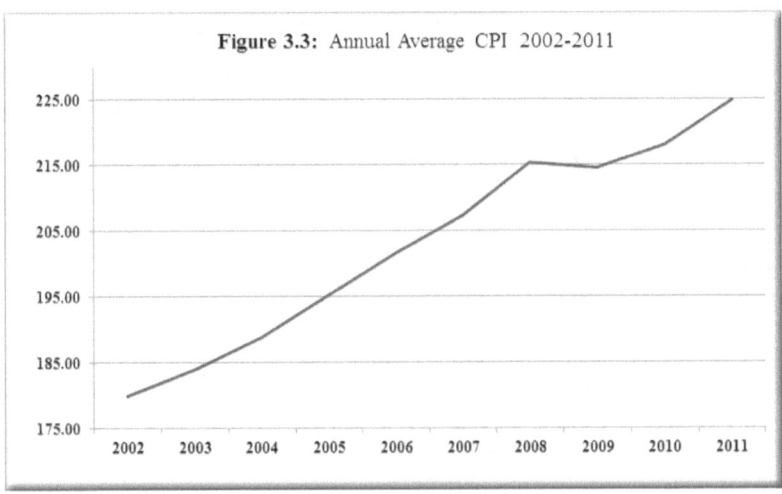

Data Source: US Bureau of Labor Statistics[12]

However, my personal observation of prices in 2012—which I will now discuss—has been that prices in key product categories are actually lower than in recent years. These prices do seem to have bottomed out, however, and have resumed inflationary trends.

Real Estate

Both residential and commercial real estate have shown signs of recovery in 2012, but sale prices of both new and existing homes remain historically—and attractively if you're an investor—low.

Cars and Trucks

Unprecedented supplies of used automobiles (coupled with high fuel prices) have driven the cost of used cars downward, while the price of new cars has remained stable or increased slightly because of increased production and transport costs. New-car prices can be expected to drop, however, once they begin to adjust for large inventories of unbought automobiles precipitated by a short supply of citizens with the capacity to buy.

Automobiles have traditionally been very expensive in most of Latin America, and Latinos will be quite pleased with the price of either a new or used car in the United States.

Gasoline and Energy Fuel

Fuel, unfortunately, is expensive everywhere—driven primarily by the price for which it can currently be sold in China. Cost savings that US citizens would expect to realize from increased supplies of fuel produced by US oil companies don't materialize because those companies can sell fuel for so much more in China. This condition aggravates Americans' already low opinion of oil companies, because the companies' profitability goes up right along with the price at the US pump. In spite of these conditions, US fuel prices remain competitive with most other countries around the world and would be perceived as low by many.

Interestingly enough, supplies of natural gas appear to be near all-time highs at the moment, which is holding down the price of heating and electricity (because electric companies supplement their power production with natural-gas-fired power plants).

Crime

Crime in the United States continues to diminish—even as national unemployment remains high and citizens' general economic frustration escalates. As shown in Table 3-1, serious crime throughout the United States has fallen in virtually every measureable category—regardless of which date-range is analyzed.

Table 3-1: FBI Crime in the United States
—Percent Change in Volume and Rate per 100,000 population—
1, 5 and 10-Year Ranges

Years	Violent Crime	Violent Crime Rate	Murder and Non-Negligent Manslaughter	Murder and Non-Negligent Manslaughter Rate	Forcible Rape	Forcible Rape Rate
2011/2010	-3.8%	-4.5%	-0.7%	-1.5%	-2.5%	-3.2%
2011/2007	-15.4%	-18.1%	-14.7%	-17.4%	-9.5%	-12.4%
2011/2002	-15.5%	-21.9%	-10.0%	-16.8%	-12.4%	-19.0%

Years	Robbery	Robbery Rate	Aggravated Assault	Aggravated Assault Rate	Property Crime	Property Crime Rate
2011/2010	-4.0%	-4.7%	-3.9%	-4.6%	-0.5%	-1.3%
2011/2007	-20.8%	-23.3%	-13.3%	-16.1%	-8.3%	-11.2%
2011/2002	-15.8%	-22.2%	-15.7%	-22.1%	-13.3%	-19.9%

Years	Burglary	Burglary Rate	Larceny-Theft	Larceny-Theft Rate	Motor Vehicle Theft	Motor Vehicle Theft Rate
2011/2010	0.9%	0.2%	-0.7%	-1.4%	-3.3%	-4.0%
2011/2007	-0.1%	-3.3%	-6.6%	-9.5%	-35.0%	-37.1%
2011/2002	1.7%	-6.0%	-12.7%	-19.3%	-42.6%	-47.0%

Source: US Federal Bureau of Investigation[13]

Violent crime in particular has declined sharply—and increasingly so—over the past several years. Figure 3-4 illustrates the rapidly declining incidence of violent crime in the United States. On a per capita basis, this decline is even more encouraging. More and more American communities are experiencing unprecedented security and freedom from violent criminals.

Figure 3-4: US Violent Crime

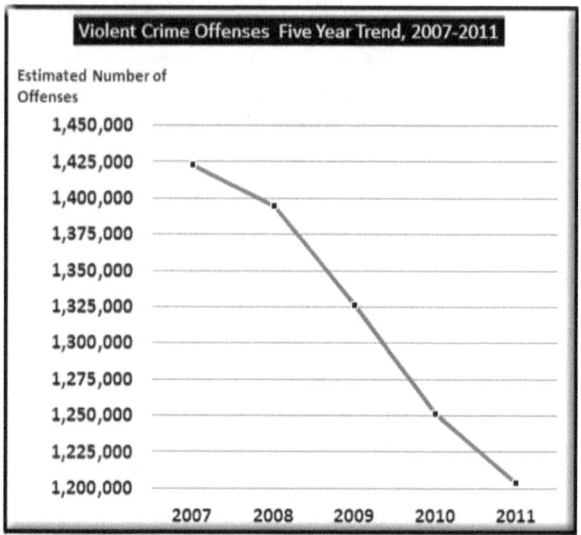

Source: *US Federal Bureau of Investigation*[14]

Property crime in the United States has also declined as illustrated in Figure 3-5; however, the rate of decline for these crimes has tapered significantly over the past few years.

Figure 3-5: US Property Crime

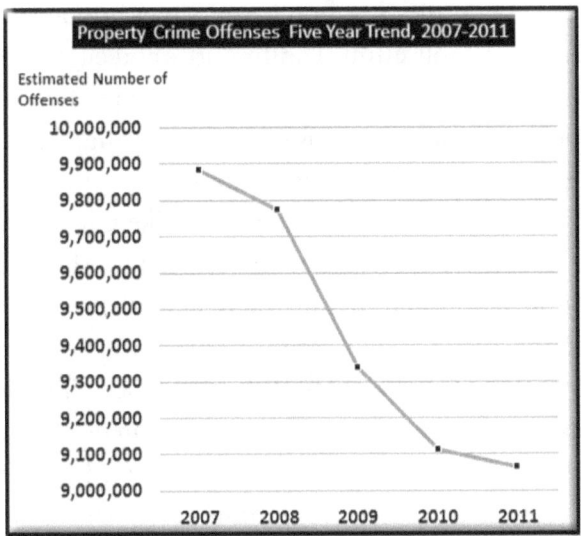

Source: *US Federal Bureau of Investigation*[15]

Crime occurs everywhere that unscrupulous people want something that other people have, and the United States is not immune to crime. While these reports clearly indicate that crime—and even violent crime—is being committed in the United States, they underscore a very encouraging trend for potential immigrants. Personal security, which has always been excellent in the United States, is getting even better.

Diverse and Secure Communities

Immigrants and nonimmigrants alike have different motivations for the communities in which they choose to live. Some prefer to immerse themselves in the new culture, determined that their family should immediately learn the local language and customs and assimilate into their new home. Others are not so confident, and they may feel a sense of trepidation and anxiety about having to adjust to the racial, cultural, and linguistic differences of a new country all at once.

The beauty of choosing the United States as a new home is that our country prides itself on being a melting pot of cultures and ethnicities. Whole ethnic communities and cities have sprung up or evolved over time throughout the United States, consisting of small pockets or large groups of foreign immigrants and other expatriates who prefer to live with fellow countrymen rather than as "islands" in a new land. Communities like Chinatown, Little Saigon, Little Cuba, Korea Town, and many others create the possibility of wading into US life incrementally.

The burgeoning US Hispanic community in particular illustrates the flexibility of these lifestyle choices. Latinos in the United States vary from 100 percent assimilated—having raised several generations of US citizens—to primarily segregated—living in 100 percent Hispanic communities that maintain their Latin American languages and cultures.

A great benefit of immigrant investment programs is that families need not live where they make their investment. This provides excellent flexibility in choosing a new community.

Education and Career Opportunities

Next to personal and financial security, education—particularly for children—remains a leading motivational factor for immigration to the United States. Excellent public schools and top-performing private schools, along with world-class private and state universities, offer some of the most attractive educational opportunities in the world. Perhaps more importantly, the supply of these opportunities—and therefore access to them—is bigger in the United States than in any other country in the world.

Immigrant investor families, even those with only conditional permanent residency, enjoy resident tuition at institutions of higher learning and free access to public schools. Frequently, immigrants also benefit from minority education programs.

After completing their education, graduates are exposed to perhaps the widest range of employment and career opportunities in the world—including an unprecedented opportunity to start their own business.

Rebound

At least as far as the US economy is concerned, unprecedented collapse is usually followed by unprecedented growth and prosperity. Since the foundation of our country in the eighteenth century, our collective failures have led to reinvention, innovation, and expansion. Mere "recovery" in the United States is rare. More often than not, our growth after a downturn far exceeds our previous economic highs. Is this economic behavior indefinitely sustainable? Perhaps not, but thus far it has been the norm, and based on US history, only a foolish gambler would bet against us.

Most US experts have declared that the 2008 economic meltdown was our worst collapse since our Great Depression. Many have suggested—since we are not fully recovered from it—that it may turn out to be even worse. It stands to reason that if an early-twentieth-century United States, devoid of all of our current resources and technology, could recover from the Great Depression and emerge from World War II with the growth and expansion that characterized the latter half of that century, that our recovery from economic difficulty with twenty-first-century resources in a truly global marketplace might dramatically surpass the most positive expectations.

Armed with a belief that the United States presents an extremely compelling investment opportunity and unparalleled quality of life, we'll take a look at what qualifies as an immigrant investment opportunity, and what specific qualities to look for in choosing the investment that's right for your family.

CHAPTER 4

Qualifying EB-5 Investments: How Do We Choose an Opportunity?

This chapter contains three separate sections related to the qualifying investment that a participating investor chooses. The specific choice of qualifying investment is the most important decision that an immigrant investor will make. The future of the investor's family may literally ride on this decision—a type of risk that even a skilled and experienced investor may not typically experience, and there is bound to be some fear associated with making it. So while these sections about the investment may seem redundant at first, the importance of making the right choice helps to rationalize that coverage. Investment criteria that USCIS examines to determine if an investment is eligible, on one hand, may also be important selection criteria that an investor reviews even more rigorously on the other hand. The management team of a given company or project, for example, will be reviewed in a cursory way by USCIS to determine its likelihood of success, while management should be examined comprehensively by an investor to optimize his confidence in the enterprise's success. By providing some detailed guidance about the types of investment and some criteria for a wise choice, I hope to instill investors with the confidence to make this decision—because the risk and dire consequences of *not* making a choice likely outweigh the potential consequences of a poor investment choice.

With regard to the EB-5 program, the investment choice is especially crucial because the failure of a company or project may result in an investor and family members losing their visas—in addition to the risk of financial loss. This book seeks to mitigate some of the fear associated with this choice. But for many investors who may not be comfortable making an investment in a new environment where they lack experience and understanding of business and market forces, I still recommend the enlistment of a trustworthy consultant or adviser who can assist the foreign investor with opportunity analysis and selection.

The first section of this chapter examines the types of investment that satisfy USCIS's requirements for the EB-5 program. This analysis considers the general characteristics of an investment opportunity and whether or not it comports with federal regulations. The second section guides the investor through an examination of more-specific investment choices—looking most closely at the probability that a given investment will create the necessary employment. Then in the third section, I'll provide some more-targeted guidance and advice on the specific criteria that an investor should use to identify an investment that not only satisfies program requirements and is likely to produce the necessary jobs, but also matches the investor's financial objectives and risk tolerance.

Choosing a Qualifying Investment

Virtually any type of business can be funded through EB-5 investment in some fashion. In this section, we will examine the few specific criteria that make a commercial enterprise or project eligible for EB-5 investment, focusing on the standard that USCIS will apply when evaluating the opportunity. Then we will turn our attention to even more specific elements that may make one opportunity more attractive than another from the *investor's* perspective. In all cases, the business or project will have to submit a comprehensive business plan and financial statements to USCIS that are tailored specifically to the EB-5 program. The tailoring that I am describing relates to expressing in detail how EB-5 investment dollars will be deployed, and how and when those investments will create jobs.

- For *direct* EB-5 investment, a company's financial plan must illustrate the projected use of investment dollars, and the operations/human resources plan must reflect what full-time jobs will be created, how many full-time employees will be hired, and when the hiring is expected to occur.
- For *regional-center* investments, the financial plan will describe in detail the use of investor funds, and the business plan may also contain information relative to job creation; however, the main job-creation explanation will appear in the comprehensive economic model.

Any direct or regional-center opportunity that does not illustrate these elements in a business plan will not be approved by USCIS as a qualified investment.

Relocation/Expansion Investments

For the right investors and for the right foreign companies, relocation or expansion of an existing foreign business into the United States may be an attractive option. Certainly any businessman might prefer to take a risk on his own efforts and his own management experience and business expertise—to be in control of how and when his investment is deployed. A business that is already doing a considerable amount of work in the United States may be an excellent candidate for a relocation or expansion investment.

I want to caution any foreign investors, however, who may be considering relocating or expanding into the United States. As we learned with my good friend Jorge, successful—even world-class—business experience in a foreign country does not necessarily translate into immediate business success in the United States.

As an example, Jorge identified what looked like an outstanding commercial real-estate opportunity just days after arriving in Idaho. The owner of a furniture factory in a rural county had gone out of business and was selling his factory, along with all of the machinery and equipment that were inside it. He was asking a very fair price, and it all seemed serendipitous—almost too good to be true. It was. By a pure stroke of luck, Jorge enquired about the zoning of the property. It turned out to be zoned by the county for agricultural purposes only. The current owner had been given permission to build a shop and to make furniture incidental to his farming business, but no other business could operate in that facility without an exhaustive and protracted rezoning process. Even if Jorge had been able to get permission to operate a new furniture factory there, reselling the property sometime in the future might be nearly impossible. He avoided this huge mistake, but just barely. He later acknowledged that he knew almost nothing about US and local real-estate rules.

All markets are different, and a foreign business leader faces significant challenges getting a business off the ground in the United States. While it can certainly be done, it will probably not be as easy and smooth a process as you expect. It may be well worth considering a partnership with existing US business owners in an industry with which you are familiar. You can always wade into establishment and ownership of your own US business at your own pace, separate from your EB-5 investment—and without the employment requirements. One of the values of working with a full-service investment-visa service provider is that these entities/individuals will be familiar with qualified and compelling companies and regional-center projects that are seeking investment. We'll discuss this type of "matchmaking" service later in the chapter and again in chapter 10.

In Jorge's own words, "If I had it to do over again, I might have invested in a regional center or another small company, and started my own business on the side. I did not expect so many regulations and administrative requirements in the US." Keep in mind that Jorge and his family had more than twenty years of very successful experience in their industry before they decided to relocate the business to the United States, and they moved to a very friendly business environment in Idaho.

A foreign entrepreneur with an idea to launch a brand-new business in the United States (such as an ethnic restaurant) will have some of these same considerations. Consider partnering with US business owners who already manage businesses of the type being considered.

Employment Creation

The number-one consideration that USCIS will have—and that investors should have—in the evaluation of any EB-5 investment opportunity is always going to be *jobs*. Employment creation will determine the success of the project, but more importantly, it will determine the ultimate reward of unconditional permanent residency and/or US citizenship. Investors who select a business or project that does not create the requisite number of jobs may face deportation from the United States along with their family members, regardless of whether or not the company pays back the investor's money. Therefore, it is vitally important that any EB-5 investment opportunity be evaluated based on the number of jobs it intends to produce, and the likelihood that it will achieve that number. A "cushion" of extra jobs will provide additional confidence to the investor.

If a company or business idea is not likely to produce a minimum of eleven full-time jobs over the ensuing two years (a 10 percent jobs cushion) per investor, then it is probably not a good fit for the EB-5 program. For example, a new software company may be innovative enough to produce outstanding software, but software companies frequently start out with only two or three software developers writing code in their home offices. It may be several years before they sell enough of their software to warrant the hiring of additional staff or developers. This type of software company would be a poor choice for EB-5 investment. On the other hand, a slightly more mature software company with good sales can grow extremely quickly and easily require far more than ten employees per investor in a very short time. Also remember, however, that software developers are going to expect higher pay. Sustaining their employment may be much more expensive and more difficult—given your investment—than restaurant employees who earn minimum wage plus tips.

So also consider that US$500,000 is not enough money to accomplish the basic operational needs of a company *and* hire and sustain the employment of ten full-time employees for two and a half years. Since most EB-5 opportunities strive for eligibility for the US$500,000 investment threshold in order to competitively attract investors, it is important to evaluate the company or project's plan and ability to use the US$500,000 investment to effectively grow the business to the point that it can sustain such employment. The presence of additional investment or debt capital from sources other than EB-5 investors can provide additional assurance that jobs will be created.

Management Team

An effective analysis of any investment opportunity includes an evaluation of the experience and track record of the company's management team. While USCIS has not positioned itself to call winners and losers among various business opportunities, they have expressed that the experience of the management team and the apparent likelihood that the managers can succeed in the proposed venture *are* criteria in the approval process.

For example, if an EB-5 investor family from Brazil has decided that they would like to open a Brazilian restaurant in Maine, but they can show no history or track record of restaurant-management experience, USCIS is unlikely to give them the opportunity to try their luck at such a business. USCIS is looking for some likelihood that the business will succeed and actually create the requisite jobs. If, on the other hand, the Brazilian family meets owners of a Brazilian restaurant and invests together with them, the proposed business is more likely to gain USCIS approval.

The case study of Tomas Menendez in Appendix C provides an excellent example. Tomas had extensive experience and success as a bar and nightclub owner in Mexico. But he readily admitted he didn't know the first thing about opening or operating a club in the United States. When he met his new partners from Texas who had many years of successful restaurant-management experience in the United States, it was clear that his likelihood of gaining USCIS approval would be increased if he invested in—and helped to manage—their Amarillo hotel project.

It is important that investors select opportunities with proven officers and managers. The success of the project, the creation of jobs, and the ultimate return of the investors' principal will largely depend on the skill and experience of the management team.

Rural Areas and TEAs

In order to qualify for a minimum investment of US$500,000, a company and its EB-5 investors must show that at the time of the investment, the project or company was located in either a rural area or a TEA. (See the section pertaining to rural areas and TEAs in chapter 2 for an explanation of these terms.) The existence or absence of TEAs may fluctuate with each quarterly unemployment analysis, and will certainly fluctuate with each decade's US Census. Similarly, areas that are, and appear to be, quite rural and desolate may be included in or absorbed into a nearby MSA.

Therefore, it is important that investors assure themselves that a company or project is indeed located in an appropriate area when the investment will be made. If a rural or TEA condition does not exist at the time of the investment, then a US$1 million investment will be required, and if commitments have been made in writing that acknowledge this possibility, then an investor may be expected (and obligated) to double-down on the investment—increasing it from US$500,000 to US$1 million.

The absence or presence of TEAs can usually be proven with either US federal labor statistics or a letter from a state government official stating that the site of the investment is a TEA at the time of the investment. Rural areas must be proven—with mapping—to be outside of any MSA and outside the boundary of a community with a population of twenty thousand or more.

Repayment of Principal

It is against the law—the regulations governing EB-5 investment—for a company, regional center, or project to promise or guarantee the repayment or reimbursement of invested principal in any way or at any time. This is the nature of at-risk investment as USCIS and the US Congress have defined it. Nevertheless, an investment opportunity's plan and its likelihood of returning EB-5 investors' money is an important consideration in the evaluation of that opportunity. The business plan and financial statements should lay out a detailed projection and timeline of the revenues, break-even point, profits, and payment of dividends and/or distributions to shareholders.

An investor should have some level of confidence in the ability of the management team to achieve these results and to at least repay the invested principal. The best EB-5 opportunities—in order to compete for investors in the marketplace—generally try to come up with a five- to seven-year repayment plan that begins reimbursing EB-5 investors in the third year of investment (after the two-year at-risk period).

Always keep in mind that the best-laid plans and financial projections can fall short of their forecasts, and repayment of principal may take much longer than the plan suggests. An investor should rationalize that, "I am getting my family to personal and financial security through permanent residency in the United States. I certainly want to get my money back, but if it takes longer than expected, that's a secondary consideration."

Return on Investment

Historically, EB-5 investment opportunities have not offered substantial return on investment (ROI) simply because the permanent resident US visa is an extremely valuable item that investors have accepted in lieu of an expectation of gains or long-term ownership positions. Frequently, EB-5 business plans have called for the "claw back" of an EB-5 investor's equity share of a company or project as their principal investment is repaid—so that five to seven years from the initial investment, the investor has received his visa, the principal has been reimbursed, and he has completely forfeited their equity position in the company.

This approach has worked well in the Chinese market where potential investors were groomed to believe—either rightly or wrongly—that the US visa was so valuable they should not expect any additional return on their investment. To be sure, EB-5 is one of only a very few ways to obtain permanent residency in the United States, especially for Chinese citizens, and it is unquestionably the fastest way. Therefore, it is quite valuable.

Nevertheless, in recent years, as the EB-5 industry has matured and has become much more competitive, regional centers and many direct-investment opportunities have begun to offer long-term ownership, preferred equity, and other ROI-based incentives to attract investors.

Simultaneously, in other EB-5 markets like Mexico—where there may be some alternative pathways to US residency—investors may have higher expectations for ROI. For these, and also for markets where the urgency or motivation to immigrate to the United States is not quite as high, projects and companies may have to offer higher returns to attract investors.

In any case, however, I would caution potential EB-5 investors to carefully evaluate any opportunity projecting very high returns on investment. These can generally be assumed to be extremely high-risk investments that must inflate projected ROIs in order to attract investor interest.

Choosing a Compelling Investment

Okay ... so now let's take a look at selecting a specific investment opportunity. This section is intended for those foreign citizens who *are not* relocating or expanding their existing foreign business into the United States or launching a new company of their own. Rather, this section will look at selection criteria for direct EB-5 investments in existing US small businesses and investments through regional centers. We will also briefly discuss investment in or purchase of troubled US businesses.

Remember that any investment that may satisfy USCIS requirements as a "qualified" investment does not necessarily indicate that the opportunity is a "good" or a "safe" investment, or that it matches your personal expertise or your family's financial goals. So examination of various investment opportunities according to the criteria in this and the following section is recommended.

We have already discussed this at length in the preceding section, but it bears repeating over and over again: if a company or regional-center project is not going to produce jobs, with at least a 10 percent surplus of projected jobs, you should not consider an investment in that commercial enterprise. Regardless of how attractive the returns or the repayment plan or the management team may be, if the company does not deliver on job creation as required by the EB-5 program, you and your family are not going to get the conditions removed from your visas and you may face deportation. This warning is not intended to discourage investors and families from participating in the EB-5 program. The program works and is proven. My purpose is simply to advise investors that they *must* evaluate job creation of a company or project above any other criteria.

So, based on all that precautionary language, let's look at businesses and regional-center projects that create jobs.

Direct Investment in Labor-Intensive Small Businesses

Don't be discouraged by the word "small." Small businesses that employ fewer than five hundred employees, and which derive less than US$20 million per year in revenue, account for more than

80 percent of US employment. A small business can have an excellent chance of producing the number of jobs that an EB-5 investor requires. The key is to look for industries and companies that are labor-intensive—requiring several people to accomplish the mission. In other words, a "by hand" auto-detailing business is going to be a better choice than a fully automated car wash. The automated car wash might be an attractive and profitable investment opportunity because it will have low labor costs, but it will almost certainly be a terrible EB-5 investment. The following is a list of labor-intensive industries, which means that they hire the most full-time employees (FTEs) for a given amount of investment (capital):[16]

- Restaurants
- Hotels/Resorts
- Retail Sales
- Agriculture/Food-Products Manufacturing
- Mining

More capital-intensive industries may make excellent EB-5 investments, but the thing to keep in mind is that the more capital—your investment—a company or project has to spend on capital-intensive operational activities, the less they will have available to achieve and sustain the employment your visa requires.

Investment in Labor-Intensive Regional-Center Projects

The same industries listed above would tend to provide excellent regional-center project investment opportunities, with the probable exception of restaurants. Only an extremely large restaurant is likely to require the kind of investment capital that a regional center typically attracts. Possible exceptions might be a Dave &

Buster's, Big Al's, or Casa Bonita type of themed restaurants or family entertainment centers that involve extremely large square footage and a massive full-time staff. Most restaurants, however, are a more appropriate fit for direct EB-5 investment.

Many regional centers promote large commercial real-estate developments that may house businesses from any or several of the labor-intensive industries. Additionally, regional centers use their economic modeling to forecast indirect and induced job creation through industry multipliers that take into account the establishment of service businesses like restaurants and movie theaters and grocery stores and the hiring that they do. This statistical analysis permits regional-center projects to benefit from a much higher total jobs output than the core business or "anchor tenant" of a development could achieve alone.

One word of caution relative to regional-center investments (and some direct investments as well): As I mentioned in the "Recent Developments" section of chapter 1, USCIS has begun to look unfavorably on the job creation of tenant occupants as opposed to the owners of the development project. In other words, some adjudicators have taken a very subjective view of an EB-5 project that builds an arena, for example, and then attempts to count the jobs of a vendor who manages the concessions at the arena. Did the developer (who may own the arena or may not) hire the full-time employees, or did the concessionaire who is actually headquartered offsite and is merely a tenant of the facility that the EB-5 investment built?

The obvious question—especially in the 2012 economy—is, "Who cares, as long as new jobs are created?" Consider a development to build a shopping mall. The shopping mall will likely hire a leasing sales team and administrative staff, and they might hire a security staff and a maintenance and cleaning crew, or they may even contract for those services. In any event, the employment of the mall itself would be marginal at best. But an effectively managed shopping mall could be responsible for literally *thousands* of jobs in the department stores, restaurants, and shops throughout the facility. USCIS has suggested that those employees—of the tenant occupants—will not be counted as direct employment. This adjustment in USCIS's view of projects and employment should be a consideration when evaluating an EB-5 investment opportunity, particularly among regional centers. Unfortunately, USCIS will provide very limited advance guidance with respect to a proposed business idea, so enterprises and investors must rely on experienced industry professionals to develop qualified projects.

Troubled US Businesses

One potential EB-5 investment would be into the revitalization or purchase of an existing troubled business. USCIS defines a troubled business as one that shows a loss, at least on paper, for the preceding two years prior to the EB-5 investment. While it is unclear in the regulation, it would appear that a troubled business could be funded either directly or via a regional center (if it is appropriately large). One potential advantage of this EB-5 investment is that a troubled business is only responsible for maintaining the employment level at the time of the investment, and then adding 40 percent more employment *or* ten employees— whichever is less—per investor, over the two and a half years following the EB-5 investment. For a small business that currently has ten employees, with only one EB-5 investor, this means only four additional employees need to be hired.

The main issue in my mind as I consider the value of investment in a troubled business is: "Why invest in a business that hasn't proven it is capable of succeeding?" Turnaround stories are great and there are great bargains among struggling businesses, but would I risk my family's wealth and our US residency on the company's ability to sustain and create jobs when the existing owners/management team haven't proven they have what it takes to survive in business?

I would urge extreme caution when considering investment in a troubled business unless the investor has considerable and specific skill and experience relative to that industry *and* is able to negotiate for a strong leadership position within the company from which to affect management change and directly influence business decisions.

Choosing an Investment That Matches You

Many affluent foreign citizens have close contacts in the United States and are able to identify or learn about investment opportunities that may qualify as EB-5 investments. Others may decide to strike out on their own and relocate/expand their existing business or launch their own idea in the United States. Many, however, who are interested in the EB-5 program may not have friends or acquaintances in the United States who can recommend investment opportunities and may also not have any business ideas of their own. This is where an EB-5 consultant firm that works with both the investors and the companies seeking investment can be extremely valuable.

Full-service EB-5 service providers identify, analyze, and assist companies that are interested in attracting EB-5 investment in getting prepared to attract investors and to gain USCIS approval. From helping a direct-investment opportunity to prepare and tailor its business plans to coaching and guiding a community through the establishment of a regional center to marketing direct-investment companies and regional-center projects abroad, EB-5 consultants are well-positioned to evaluate and recognize the best and most prepared investment opportunities. Investors are well-advised to seek these professionals out and to rely on their experience and contacts to identify a qualified EB-5 investment opportunity. A seasoned EB-5 consultant typically works with a diverse portfolio of companies and regional centers and is very likely to have an opportunity that matches an investor's interests and investment goals.

In this section, I'll provide some general advice about how to select a qualified EB-5 investment that matches your investment objectives. Once you understand the EB-5 program and what qualifies as an eligible investment—and even if you have the assistance of an experienced EB-5 service provider—you will still need to find an investment that fits with your knowledge and experience and matches your immigration and financial goals.

Jobs, Jobs, Jobs

Okay, okay ... I won't be *labor* this point again (pun intended), but this must always be the number-one evaluation factor of any EB-5 investment opportunity for all of the reasons we have already covered repeatedly *and* because you should only be comfortable with an investment that is going to result in an unconditional visa.

Understanding/Comfort

An investor should always understand the business and industry into which he or she is placing an investment and be comfortable with that choice. A woman who grew up studying math and science and who has expertise in chemical engineering may know absolutely nothing about the restaurant business or the hospitality industry, even though she may be great at picking a terrific restaurant or hotel. This woman would not be expected to understand the restaurant business or to be comfortable monitoring the performance of a restaurant. Therefore, she probably should not invest in a restaurant, particularly with a large portion of her net worth and her family's US residency riding on such an investment. Similarly, a lifelong restaurateur would probably not fully understand or be comfortable with a commercial real-estate project to build a professional basketball arena.

Look for investment opportunities in businesses and industries with which you are familiar, that you at least generally understand, and that you agree with morally. For example, if you can't stand the petroleum industry because you think they are profit-hungry and environmentally unconscious, then why in the world would you invest in a regional center that is drilling oil wells? Chances are you neither understand that industry nor agree with it morally, so it would be a poor investment choice.

Risk Tolerance

Private Placement Memoranda and subscription agreements should contain harsh, discouraging language and data about the risk of an EB-5 investment opportunity and investors' potential to lose all of their investment. These warnings should be taken seriously. Although risk is an unavoidable factor in any investment, and investors and investees will both take measures to minimize and mitigate risk, the investor must still have a tolerance and an ability to absorb any potential loss as a result of the investment.

Offering documents that ask you to make an investment of half a million dollars or more without any guarantee or even a possibility of reimbursement for more than two years and *then* speak of the possibility of mandatory capital calls should be avoided as EB-5 investments. These "opportunities" are actually expanding your risk so that you can lose more than everything you invest, and frequently they offer little or no potential return on your investment—returns you would typically expect from a higher-risk investment.

Sometimes Higher Risk Means More Control

One of the requirements of the EB-5 Immigrant Investor Program is that investors must occupy a managerial, decision-making role in the company receiving their investment. This can be satisfied by a voting board of directors seat, even though that position may not confer any day-to-day management authority. In a regional-center investment, where investors frequently become voting directors in a limited partnership (LP) that has very little actual equity—and very little managerial influence—in the actual project, investors give up a lot of control over the use of their investment dollars. Risk for the project is shared among many EB-5 investors in the LP and with domestic investors in the project, and therefore there is a general sense that control is traded for some reduction in risk.

This is similar to the mentality of a mutual-fund investment, where many investors have virtually no control at all in the operation of the companies into which they invest or even in the trading actions of the fund manager; but the risk is also reduced, as well as the cost of investment into such a great portfolio of companies.

Investors who are comfortable with more risk but are not comfortable with a complete loss of control may prefer direct EB-5 investment in a small company that is willing to defer to more of the investor's judgment and managerial guidance. This is particularly true if an investor has specific experience or expertise relative to the invested industry (a foreign doctor investing in a private health-care practice, for example). Such an investor may be given not only a voting director seat but a paid executive-officer position in the company. Certain investors are willing to take on some additional risk in order to have more managerial control.

Management-Team Track Record

We discussed the importance of a good management team in the first section of this chapter. USCIS is going to evaluate the likelihood that the business has at least *some* chance of succeeding and creating jobs, and it will evaluate the experience of the management team. You should too. A track record of success in growing companies—especially in the specific industry of the business seeking your investment—elevates your chance of success in the EB-5 program.

Similarly, if you happen to be contemplating an investment in a regional center, a track record of success in attracting, processing, and getting unconditional visas for investors is an important factor to consider. While there are still only a few regional centers that have led investors through the entire EB-5 process, and you may not be attracted to those specific investment opportunities, you should at least look for *some* level of EB-5-specific experience and/or partnership with service providers/attorneys who do have a track record of EB-5 success.

If you are the type of person who is interested in EB-5 investment for the safety and financial security of your family, but you have no interest in or experience with investment, then I absolutely recommend that you only consider investment with a regional center that has actually processed EB-5 investors all the way through the process. There are just too many other risk factors to which an inexperienced investor will be exposed—so they should at least mitigate the risk associated with the immigration process. For example, a twenty- or thirty-something single mother—such as Regina Velazquez in the second case study in Appendix C—who has inherited money from her deceased husband or another relative but has limited business education and virtually no experience with investment would be well-advised to confine her selection to regional centers with proven USCIS track records.

In Regina's case, she chose to invest in a senior assisted-living regional center—not because she had any knowledge or understanding of that industry, but because she was confident that the owners did and because the regional center had a strong track record of getting visas approved. Plus, she felt good about helping senior citizens.

Hopefully, the fear of choosing the wrong investment will not discourage an investor from getting her family to a secure new home in the United States, but she can at least reduce some of the anxiety of the immigration process. For this type of investor, the track record and management team of the company receiving the investment becomes one of the prime evaluation criteria.

Repayment Plan/Return on Investment

Every investor will hope to at least recover his or her invested principal. An EB-5-eligible investment opportunity should have a clearly defined plan and timeline for repaying principal. In order to be competitive with other EB-5 opportunities, most companies/projects have laid out a five- to seven-year plan. While this is not a guarantee of reimbursement by any means—which would be specifically forbidden by the rules of the program—a thoughtful and carefully designed repayment plan is evidence that the managers have scheduled principal repayment into their business and financial models. If the repayment plan seems ambiguous—or of secondary importance to the management team—then it probably is.

As discussed previously, EB-5 investment opportunities have historically offered very low or no return on investment (ROI) or long-term ownership opportunities—largely because the EB-5 visa itself is such a valuable incentive. However, as the investment-visa industry becomes more competitive and EB-5 opportunities begin to offer ROI to attract more investors, potential investors should beware of opportunities offering extremely high returns. These would tend to indicate an investment opportunity that has extremely high risk and has to lure investors (victims) using ROI figures that they are very unlikely to achieve.

In any case, ROI should be a lower priority concern in evaluating any EB-5 opportunity than job creation, immigration experience/track record, management-team experience, and safety of principal.

Administrative Fees

EB-5 investment opportunities are likely to require administrative fees. These fees are used by regional centers and direct-investment companies to pay for investor processing and documentation, to defray their own administrative costs, and for a number of other purposes. It is important to understand not only the amount of the administrative fee but what is included in that amount.

For example, some regional centers do not pay any USCIS filing or processing fees out of investor administrative fees collected. These fees would need to be paid to USCIS by the investor. Other regional centers do include USCIS charges in the administrative fee. Some regional centers may include all expenses associated with the I-526 process but not the I-829 process. Be sure that you understand how much or how little of the USCIS process will be paid through your administrative fee.

Generally speaking, administrative and operational costs of a regional center may not be derived from the EB-5 investment funds, and neither may immigration expenses of the investors, so these must be paid either directly by the investor or through administrative fees paid to the regional center or commercial enterprise.

Some EB-5 investment opportunities compensate their

marketing partners with finder's fees and commissions and offset other marketing costs using funds collected under administrative fees. This is permitted if managed in accordance with US securities regulations, and generally speaking, an investment opportunity should be expected to disclose this use of administrative fees.

Location of the Investment Relative to Your Residence

Many investors have become comfortable placing investments in companies that are headquartered in faraway cities or even overseas. While this should not be a high-priority factor in evaluating an investment opportunity, some investors may wish to live close to where their money is invested. Since the EB-5 program is such a personal program—having living and residency implications for investors and not just financial implications—investors may feel quite a bit more comfortable being able to readily contact and communicate with project or company managers. They may wish to attend board meetings in person and closely monitor the progress of the company.

In this case, investors have two choices: Either invest in the community where they hope to live or choose a home in the community where they make their investment. Since there is a much larger selection of choices for homes than there is for qualified EB-5 investment opportunities, most investors will have better luck identifying the investment they want to make and then finding a home near that company or regional-center project. Not all major cities have qualified EB-5 investment opportunities yet (although they should), so investors who have their heart set on living in a particular place may have to resign themselves to being invested in a distant company or project.

Having discussed the vital selection criteria and characteristics of solid immigrant investment opportunities, we move on in chapter 5 to the specific process prospective investors must follow.

CHAPTER 5

The EB-5 Process for Investors: How Do We Make This Happen?

The EB-5 investment process is onerous but not necessarily complicated. It takes considerable effort and time, but the pathway toward a visa is relatively clear. In this chapter, we will discuss four important but simple steps that investors should take to ensure success:

1. Prepare
2. Invest
3. Apply
4. Relocate

Appendix A includes three checklists that provide additional step-by-step guidance for investors, depending on whether they are relocating their own business, making a direct EB-5 investment, or investing in a regional center.

Step 1: Prepare

There is significant preparation to do in anticipation of making an immigrant investment. Step 1 includes all of the planning and document-gathering activities, as well as the identification and recruitment of various service providers.

Make a Plan

Begin by writing down the steps highlighted in this chapter and then breaking down each of the steps into easily achievable segments. Assign a schedule—projected dates of accomplishment—to each step and segment.

Start Gathering Documents Today!

Even if you are not yet sure that you want to immigrate and make an EB-5 investment, you will save a lot of time and effort later if you begin the process of gathering, copying, and translating all of the necessary documents. It will likely take several weeks to gather, copy, organize, and translate all of the documents required by the EB-5 program. Finding a certified translator who wants the necessary volume of work may take some time as well. Obviously, if you happen to be a citizen of a country where original governmental documents have been produced in English (such as Singapore or India), then you are at a distinct advantage.

You will need at least four copies of each document plus translations, and while the original documents need not be submitted to USCIS, they should be kept together and easily accessible in case they are needed for a live interview.

It should also be noted that the I-526 petition only includes information for the investor. However, after it is approved, documents for the spouse and dependent children will be required rapidly. Therefore, it is best to begin gathering all necessary documents at the same time.

The following documents should be gathered, copied, and submitted to a certified English translator for translation (if needed):

- Personal identification documents for investor, spouse, and unmarried children under twenty-one years of age at the time of petition:
- Passports and any existing US visas and entry/work permits
- Birth certificates
- Marriage licenses and divorce certificates
- School completion certificates/diplomas

Note: It might be a good idea to gather children's school transcripts at this point as well, particularly for high-school and college students.

- Business documents (especially for investors intending to relocate or expand existing foreign businesses in the United States, but also to demonstrate legitimate funding sources):
- Business licenses/permits
- Business formation/registration documents (corporation, LLC, LP, etc.)
- Business plans
- Business financial statements
- Payroll tax documents
- Pay stubs
- Personal and business financial documents:
- Bank statements (five years, at least quarterly)
- Tax returns and other tax records (preceding five years)
- Deeds/titles/bills of sale to property or other assets that are sold to derive investment funds
- Loan documents for any investment money that has been borrowed

- Affidavits/attestations by people who have given personal gifts of investment monies and the source of those funds
- Bank and other documents that track the path of funds from all sources to the US investment
- Translator's certification document/affidavit
- Police background investigation for each family member

An investor can visit the USCIS website (http://www.uscis.gov) and gather the appropriate application forms and instructions, starting with the I-526 and I-829 petitions. Investors or family members who have been admitted to the United States under another status may also require an I-485 Application to Register Permanent Residence or Adjust Status. It is recommended that even though an investor and family members may rely on the services of an immigration attorney or some other service provider, they should thoroughly read and understand all of the official immigration documents. It may be possible to locate translated copies of forms and instructions in the native language of the investor; however, USCIS does not provide them. Signed English documents will be required and will have legal standing in each EB-5 case.

Identify and Hire Service Providers

The EB-5 program and other immigration programs were intended and written for foreign nationals who barely speak or understand English. While the rules and regulations pertaining to these programs can be intimidating and appear complicated, the process is not intended to require hundreds of billable hours of work by a seasoned immigration attorney. The forms are designed so that immigrants can complete them on their own. I am not an immigration attorney, yet I have successfully completed hundreds of pages of immigration documents for my own family and for families that I have helped through my business. If I can manage this process, then I would assume that any reasonably educated person should be able to do the same.

Having said all that, the EB-5 program is a particularly complicated and at times convoluted immigration program. Its processes are pretty straightforward, and it is possible to struggle through them without the assistance of legal professionals. However, if you make any serious mistake, correcting that mistake can cost weeks or even months of unnecessary delays, and may indeed require the services of a specialized attorney who can cost thousands of dollars—if and only if they have time to take your case. Even a small mistake on an EB-5 petition or in an evidentiary document can cost weeks of delays in the Request for Evidence (RFE) process.

It may also be very useful to have an experienced immigration attorney physically submit your immigration petitions and represent your family in correspondence and interviews with USCIS and perhaps even the US State Department (consulate). This is facilitated by USCIS's G-28 Notice of Entry of Appearance as Attorney or Accredited Representative, or the G-28I form for international attorneys.[17]

Therefore, I strongly recommend that anyone considering an EB-5 investment secure the services of either an experienced immigration attorney with specific experience with the EB-5 program or an EB-5 consulting firm or other service provider that either has that same level of experience, employs an EB-5 experienced attorney, or works in partnership with an experienced immigration attorney.

Concierge-type consulting firms can add significant value to your immigration experience because they generally work with experienced attorneys, but also because they offer services and work with partners in other industries—such as real estate, banking, investments, business development, education, and state and local government—which may be incredibly useful to you and your family as you work through the immigration and relocation process. Many of these firms also employ former government managers and staffers—such as former USCIS adjudicators or administrators—who may be even more-intimately familiar with USCIS forms and processes, and what types of information may gain USCIS approval.

Such a firm can also frequently provide a savings on some of the legal costs because, while they utilize an attorney for reviewing and filing petitions and support documents, they use their own experienced staff for the rudimentary tasks of completing applications and copying, translating, and compiling documents. These services may cost significantly more if performed or contracted by an attorney. For example, at my company—Inversión Consultant Services—we work with investors to prepare the entire EB-5 petition package before submitting it to one of our attorneys for review and submission to USCIS—saving hundreds of dollars' worth of billable hours.

Step 2: Invest

The second step for immigrant investors is to actually choose an investment opportunity and to place their investments.

Identify and Choose Your Investment

In order to submit an I-526 visa petition, you must have already made a qualified EB-5 investment in a US commercial enterprise. If you are expanding, relocating, or establishing your own business, then you must submit proof to USCIS that the business has been registered and licensed in a US community and that investment funds or other assets totaling the minimum EB-5 investment amount have been transferred under the control of that business.

If you are making a direct EB-5 investment into a small US company or a regional center, then similarly, you must show that funds have been transferred to a bank account in the name of that entity—although the account may be an escrow or trust account that reverts the money back to you in the event that your visa petition is denied.

Therefore, since the I-526 document must include proof that the investment has already been made, Step 2 in the process is to identify what investment you would like to make, and then to actually make the investment. We discussed extensively in chapter 4 what constitutes a good, qualified investment for EB-5 purposes.

If you are experienced and comfortable evaluating investment opportunities, particularly in the United States, then you can undertake the process of identifying and analyzing regional centers and direct investments yourself. On the other hand, if you would not be comfortable locating or evaluating EB-5 investment opportunities, then this is another area where the enlistment of qualified assistance—a third-party service provider—may be useful. As mentioned in chapter 4, full-service immigrant-investment service providers will be familiar with qualified and attractive EB-5 investment opportunities throughout the United States and can likely recommend an investment that matches your industry tastes, your risk tolerance, and your investment goals. We will provide some guidance for identifying and selecting such a service provider in chapter 10.

Step 3: Apply

Step 3 in the investment-visa process is the formal application to the US government. Here we will assemble the visa petition and submit it to USCIS—either directly or through an immigration service provider.

Assemble and Complete the I-526 Petition

This process can be completed by the investor, a representative attorney, or another EB-5 service-provider firm. It consists of completing the I-526 form and compiling the evidentiary supporting documents—along with the petition form itself—into a well-organized, tabbed format that will facilitate the USCIS adjudicator who reviews it.

If a direct EB-5 investment is being made, the petition package will need to include the business plan of the commercial enterprise and financial projections—both tailored specifically to the EB-5 program—along with any signed subscription, operating, and/or partnership agreements, Private Placement Memoranda, escrow agreements (if applicable), and other legal documents. The package should also include—either in the business plan or separately—evidence of the rural or TEA status of the specific location of the investment, unless the investment is for US$1 million or more.

If you are investing in the relocation or expansion of an existing foreign business, include an English copy of the company's business plan and financial documents—again, tailored for the EB-5 program. An operating agreement will need to be included that identifies the ownership and managerial position of the EB-5 investor and any other investors in the company—both before and after it relocates to the United States.

If you are investing in an EB-5 regional center, you'll need to include a copy of the regional-center USCIS approval letter, along with copies of the signed legal/offering documents listed above. Remember that a regional center's project business plan and financials have been preapproved, so there is no need to remit them.

Remember to include a certified translation of any document originally produced in a language other than English, along with a copy of each original document (don't send only the translations).

An experienced US immigration attorney would likely advise you to send as little information as possible to get approved and no more, so as not to stir up questions and additional inquiry through the RFE process. This is excellent advice; however, it takes a very wise and experienced attorney or consultant to strike the proper balance in this regard. If you are not working with such a qualified professional, it is better to send all the information an adjudicator may need to render a decision without many RFEs—but to organize the petition package with extreme care so that the reviewers can find all of the information.

I personally recommend binding and tabbing the petition package in distinct sections that divide the document groups and provide clear tables of contents. A clear and comprehensive cover letter that acts as an "executive summary" of the entire petition package must also be included. In some cases, a cover letter by the investor and another by the representative attorney is appropriate.

Finally, I have been asked many times whether to include governmental support documents—whether that carries any weight in getting a petition approved. I would say that letters from government officials—such as a big-city mayor, or a governor, or a US congressman—addressed "To Whom it May Concern," stating that the official has knowledge of the business and is supportive of the development and the investor's investment, and describing how the required job creation is going to be advantageous to the community—may show the adjudicator that the investor and the target business have partnered with their community and their government agencies, and *may* carry some weight with USCIS. I certainly don't believe that such a letter can hurt the cause of the petition.

On the other hand, I doubt very much that letters from foreign government officials will add any value at all. USCIS is not likely to be interested in what any foreign official might have to say about the investor, and such a character reference is unnecessary. Also, letters from high-ranking government officials addressed directly to USCIS, State Department, or Homeland Security officials may have an unintended adverse effect on the adjudication process because a US official will be required to stop what they are doing and respond to the US bigwig personally. This tactic tends to exasperate government-agency officials and should be used very sparingly and only with great discretion.

Submit the I-526 Petition to USCIS

When the package is complete, it will likely be many hundreds of pages and nearly fill a file box, especially if you use binders to organize the documents. Make sure you and your spouse have signed the petition where designated. Include the appropriate filing fee (US$1,500 as of this writing) in the form of a cashier's check drawn on a US banking institution. I also recommend paying for "premium processing" (an additional US$1,225) using the I-907 application. Premium processing requires that USCIS render its first response within fourteen days of receiving the petition. While this does not reflect on whether the response will be negative, affirmative, or an RFE, it does seem to move the process along, even on future RFEs.

The full petition should be boxed with appropriate protective packing materials and sent via UPS or FedEx to the California Service Center of USCIS (where all EB-5 cases are received and adjudicated). Request a notice of signed receipt, and be sure to insure the package for a value of at least US$500—a minimum of what it would likely cost to produce a second copy. Check with your banker, but I don't believe there is a need to insure cashier's checks. If they are lost or stolen, the bank should be able to stop payment on them and issue replacements.

A word of caution to investors/attorneys who will be shipping from abroad: When you insure the package, you will be assigning a value to its contents. Even though the package has no commercial value, FedEx and UPS don't provide a way to distinguish between the insured value of the contents and the fact that they have no commercial value. Therefore, some customs agents may still feel that some kind of import duty or tax is owed. I advise that you simply be prepared to pay the tax and, in fact, just pay it in advance. It is better to either pay the tax or have FedEx/UPS send you a refund of the payment than to have your immigration documents tied up in customs for weeks while they sort things out with you and the shipper. You may want to write "Immigration Documents" in big bold letters all over the outside of the box, but that may have little or no effect. Alternatively, you can work with a US attorney or consulting firm that gathers all of your materials incrementally and systematically via mail and e-mail and then submits them to USCIS from a US address, avoiding this potential delay and headache altogether.

Step 4: Relocate

The final step in the investment-visa process is relocation of your family and assets to the United States. This could be a topic for an entire book of its own, and the steps and requirements may vary dramatically depending on the country from which your family is immigrating. The following represents some general recommendations.

Acquire Passports

If birth certificates were utilized for dependent children in lieu of passports in the visa petition process, then you should secure passports for those children once visas are approved and prior to relocation to the United States.

Obtain Visitors' Visas

You may want to visit the United States prior to your final visa approval in order to investigate various communities where you might want to live. To do so, you will need to secure visitors' visas (either B-1 or B-2) for yourself and any family members who will accompany you, unless you already have some other approved US status.

Secure a Residence

You will need to establish a residence as one of the requirements of the EB-5 program. You and your family can either lease or purchase a home, and it is recommended that you work with qualified real-estate service providers in the United States to assist you with this transaction. Renters' and home-ownership laws in the United States may differ significantly from your home country.

Enroll Children in School

The priority of this step may be different depending on the time of year, but particularly if fall is approaching, you may want to enroll your children in primary or secondary schools in your chosen community. University admissions usually take place the prior spring, with registration in the late summer.

Move Belongings

The final step in the relocation process should be to enlist a reliable transport service for your family's personal and household items. This should be undertaken only after the investment visa has been awarded. While Canadian, Mexican, and Central American citizens may be able to accomplish this move over roads and highways, the reliability and security of doing so may cause many to consider some combination of sea, rail, and over-the-road transport. Air cargo is also an option for some shipments.

Remember, as you work your way through the steps, refer to the checklist provided in Appendix A that corresponds with your investment situation.

Now that you're familiar with the four steps, we'll move on to the next chapter and study USCIS and how it will administer your visa petition.

CHAPTER 6

USCIS: Who Decides If We Get a Visa and How Long Will it Take?

The United States Citizenship and Immigration Services (USCIS), an agency within the US Department of Homeland Security (DHS), administers all immigration programs in the United States. The EB-5 program is administered by the California Service Center (CSC) within the Service Center Operations (SCOps) Directorate. EB-5 is governed by Codified Federal Regulation 8 CFR 204.6 and further regulated by the Immigration and Nationality Act Section 203(b) and 8 CFR 216.6.[18] In this chapter, I will present an overview of USCIS as it pertains to investment-visa programs and illustrate the process by which visa petitions will be adjudicated by this governing agency.

An EB-5 case—beginning with the I-526 Immigration Petition for Alien Entrepreneur—is reviewed by a USCIS adjudicator at the CSC. While I have met with adjudicators at USCIS outreach events and have personally verified that they have names, they are officially addressed by their duty-officer numbers, which is all you will know them by in their correspondence. Keep in mind that a duty officer who responds to one of your e-mail inquiries may not be the same one with whom you speak on another occasion. The duty officer who is the adjudicator assigned to your particular case may not always be the one who communicates with you or responds to your questions.

Summary Review/Receipt Acknowledgment

Once your I-526 petition reaches the CSC, it will be summarily reviewed for content, and if all the necessary elements appear to be in order, a receipt acknowledgment letter (Form I-797 Notice of Action)—which includes your receipt number—will be sent within a few days of USCIS receiving the package. You will need the receipt number to refer to your case anytime you or your representative attorney corresponds with USCIS.

If you have paid for premium processing (recommended), you should expect to have an initial response from USCIS within two weeks of the date on your I-797 receipt notice. That response can be an approval, a denial, or a request for additional information known as a Request for Evidence (RFE). Approvals are rare in this first response, but they do happen if the petition and support documents are all presented correctly and are well-organized. Denials are also rare for initial replies, because USCIS is more inclined to request clarification on a point than to issue an immediate denial. However, if USCIS discovers a blatantly dishonest response or some irreparable discrepancy or ineligibility in the petition during the first two-week review, it will issue a denial. Probably 90 percent of the time, the initial response for premium processing will be an RFE.

If you did not pay for premium processing, your petition is at the mercy of the CSC's case prioritization system and subject to any backlog of non-premium-processing petitions. USCIS and the CSC have devised a system for prioritizing the work of their adjudicators based not only on the order petitions were received but on the relative urgency and type of the petition. Premium processing does not necessarily override the urgency of some petitions, but not paying for premium processing guarantees that your petition will not be moved ahead of any other work the adjudicators face—unless some special order is given to reduce the backlog of EB-5 petitions specifically.

Therefore, non-premium-processing cases should not expect to get an initial response from USCIS for at least six weeks from the date of the I-797 receipt acknowledgment—and often it will take much longer than that. Don't believe for a second that the extra time it takes USCIS to respond will mean an increase in the likelihood of an approval or that the adjudicator has had more time to review your case. The adjudicator has probably not looked at your petition any longer than he or she would have for a premium processing case. It merely sat on a desk longer before he or she picked it up. The vast majority of initial responses are still RFEs.

The Request for Evidence Process

USCIS progresses through adjudication of visa petitions using its RFE process. While an extremely well-organized petition—with all of its necessary support documents neatly and accurately included—may occasionally earn an approval from USCIS on its first review, this is rare. Even if a petition is in perfect order, the petitioner may still get an RFE if an adjudicator is new or overlooks something.

Be prepared to receive and respond to RFEs that request information that was clearly included with the original petition, or with a response to a prior RFE. It is important when this happens to remain calm and respectful and to dutifully point out the specific location in the materials where the information was included. This is one of the reasons I like to use line numbers on any element of the petition I can—so that I can respectfully reply something like, "As was noted on line number 34 in the third paragraph on page 4 of the blue tab #3 section of the green binder #2 entitled 'Personal Identification Documents' …"

Each RFE usually allows the applicant approximately ninety days to submit the requested information. However, if a respondent takes the full ninety days each time he or she receives an RFE, this can severely drag out the total approval time for the petition. Therefore, it is important to respond as quickly as possible while still thoroughly and accurately answering USCIS's questions. Remember also that if a question in the RFE is not clear, contact USCIS as quickly as possible by e-mail to get clarification so that time is not wasted gathering and preparing information that is not needed.

An RFE response should be accompanied by a detailed cover letter from the applicant or representative that summarizes the response, as well as tabbed sections if there is more than one question in the RFE.

Remember that this is a US federal government process. It comes with a generous dose of bureaucracy and red tape. Generally speaking, if you patiently wade all the way through the process, you will eventually be approved. Your experience may be different from other applicants you may know who were approved faster or slower than you.

Denial

If your petition is denied, it is important that you review the denial notice and the reason for denial carefully. If the denial is because of some omission, or some piece of evidence that you failed to provide or USCIS believes you failed to provide, you may be able to reopen your case and submit the missing information. The same is true if USCIS misinterpreted a piece of information you provided or a representation you made.

However, if you have been denied for a just cause—such

as USCIS was not satisfied that the source of your investment funds was legitimate, or they discovered some criminal activity in your record that you failed to disclose—then you have very little recourse. While USCIS does have an Administrative Appeals Office, it has a dismal record of reversing adjudicators' rulings.

If you feel strongly that your petition has been incorrectly rejected, and you have the means and the time to fight the denial, then your best course of action is to file an administrative appeal—in spite of the likelihood that it will be denied—and then file a claim in US federal court. These lawsuits have had slightly more success at reversing a USCIS decision, but they are costly and can take years to resolve.

I recommend in the case of denial that you simply take your medicine, recover your investment dollars, and look for some other remedy to the situation that motivated you to immigrate.

Approval

Approximately 85 percent of all filed I-526 petitions receive approval. When USCIS approves a petition, it notifies the investor and his or her representative via an I-797B approval notice. USCIS will also notify the US Department of State so that a consular office in the investor's home country can schedule an interview. If the investor and family are already living in the United States under some other approved status, then the consular interview will be scheduled at a State Department or USCIS office near their US home. The consular interview is usually scheduled within a few weeks, but they have been known to take several months—depending on the home country of the investor, the backlog at that consular facility, and the familiarity of its staff with the EB-5 program.

It is at the consular interview that the conditional permanent resident visa is issued to the investor and the investor's immediate family. While more than 95 percent of approved EB-5 investors pass their consular interview, it is also the last opportunity for something to go wrong—for the petitioner or spouse to say something or submit some piece of evidence that results in the denial of the visa. For example, the State Department or USCIS, in the weeks leading up to the consular interview, might discover that the investor committed a crime that was not reported; or at the interview, one of the investor's teenage children might make a threatening, subversive comment about the US president. It is important for the investor family to exemplify model citizenship at the consular interview.

Once the conditional visa is approved and presented to the family, they enjoy all of the rights of any permanent resident in the United States, including the right to work and earn income, purchase property, open bank accounts, and obtain drivers' licenses and social security cards. Many US states even permit permanent residents to own and carry firearms. Check all of the applicable laws of the state where you intend to reside.

While I certainly congratulate any family that obtains a conditional permanent resident visa and encourage them to enjoy their new rights and freedoms, remember that a great deal of your time during the next two years should be spent ensuring that your investment is properly deployed and that ten permanent full-time jobs are created by your investment.

USCIS and the I-829 Petition

Within ninety days of the second anniversary of your conditional visa, you must submit your I-829 Petition by Entrepreneur to Remove Conditions—along with a new US$3,835 filing and biometric fee. USCIS will carefully review the evidence that you and/or your regional center submit to prove the proper placement of your investment and the required resultant job creation.

If you relocated your own foreign company or made a direct EB-5 invest in a US small business, then you will need to provide verifiable evidence that ten new direct full-time employees are working for the firm at the time of the I-829 submission. Acceptable evidence may include I-9 Employment Eligibility Verification forms, payroll records, payroll tax submissions, and the like.

If you invested through a regional center, then the regional center will be responsible for providing you and USCIS with evidence that the investment described in the project's economic model was actually made in the time frame, the communities, and the industries called for in the model. If the project has deviated from the model or the original business plan, and did not submit an amended project application, then the regional center must use other means to prove that significant numbers of direct jobs were created and that applicable industry multipliers result in sufficient total jobs—direct, indirect, and induced—being created.

If the resultant jobs for each investor do not reach ten, then the investor, the commercial enterprise, or the regional center must submit a plan to USCIS suggesting how and when those jobs are likely to be created. If USCIS believes that the plan to create the jobs is plausible, then they will approve the I-829 petition and award the unconditional visa. However, if they do not agree that the plan will produce the jobs, or if no plan is submitted, then the I-829 will be denied and the investor family may face removal proceedings.

This chapter has outlined the USCIS adjudication procedure. In chapter 7, we will summarize a few of the tax concepts and implications of immigrant investment.

CHAPTER 7

Immigration and Taxation: Can We Still Run Our Business in Our Home Country?

The rules, regulations, and bureaucracy that govern taxation in the United States could (and do) fill entire libraries of books. The additional content necessary to cover international tax law renders ridiculous any effort to encapsulate the tax implications that immigrant investors will face. There are trained professionals who assume the risk of guiding investors and immigrants as it pertains to tax law. In this chapter, we will attempt nothing more than to scratch the surface of the tip of the iceberg called taxation.

Disclaimer

I will preface this chapter by disclaiming that: *I am not a tax professional, nor a tax attorney, nor are any of my companies licensed tax-accounting or tax-law firms. The comments relative to US/international taxation contained in this section—and throughout this book—are general in nature, and are only my observations during my experience with investment-visa programs. These comments must not be construed as tax or legal advice, and may not reflect the actual tax regulations of either the United States or any foreign country at the time this book is* read. *Therefore, it is critically important that foreign investors—and US companies hoping to attract them—consult with a licensed tax professional or tax attorney with specific, international tax-law experience.*

The Spirit of the Program

The EB-5 program is an immigrant program. It is not a dual-citizenship or dual-residency program. There can be severe immigration and taxation consequences for intentionally or unintentionally misusing or abusing the EB-5 program relative to its intent. The program is intended for foreign citizens who wish to immigrate to the United States and to obtain permanent residency.

While it is expected that EB-5 investors and their families may wish to travel to and from their home country regularly—either to visit family and friends, for vacations, or to manage business affairs—the underlying intent of the program is that EB-5 investors and their families will reside in the United States. Family members' entries and exits will be monitored by USCIS and the US State Department (consulate) and the aggregate total of time spent in the United States by each family member must be a minimum of six months each year. For practical purposes—until the conditions are removed from the EB-5 visa through the I-829 process—it is not a good idea for a family member's time outside the United States to even approach six months. The appearance of dual residency may reflect poorly on the applicant's I-829 petition.

Immigration Implications

Remember that if an I-829 petition is denied, an EB-5 investor and his or her family will likely face removal proceedings (deportation).

Once an I-829 petition has been approved, the monitoring of entries and exits will likely continue, however enforcement relative to time in country may tend to relax somewhat. (USCIS, US

Immigration and Customs Enforcement, and the State Department have bigger immigration problems than permanent residents who overstay their visits to foreign countries.) Nevertheless, permanent residents may technically forfeit their residency if they reside outside the United States for more than half of any given year.

Investors who are interested in carrying on a more or less binational business or investment relationship with the United States, and still wish to own a home in the United States where their family can live, may wish to consider some other business or investment-visa program such as E-1 or E-2. These programs do not have the same immigration or tax implications as EB-5 because the investor and his or her family do not become permanent residents of the United States.

Tax Implications

There are monumental tax implications and consequences associated with immigration to the United States, particularly for wealthy foreign citizens. There can be outstanding opportunities for tax shelter attached to this move, but there can also be dire pitfalls if mistakes are made. This chapter will not go into detail on either the opportunities or the pitfalls. Simply be advised that the immigration process should be approached with careful and diligent tax planning by experienced tax professionals—both accountants and attorneys—in the United States and in the investor's home country. There are various accounting and tax activities that should be undertaken prior to, during, and after the investor-family's expatriation. In addition to worldwide income, there may be estate, trust, gift, inheritance, and capital-gains tax issues associated with the immigration activity.[19]

It is highly advisable that the services of an investor's foreign tax professional be coordinated with a US tax expert specifically experienced in immigration and EB-5 issues. While I'm no fan of paying money to attorneys for work I can do myself, there are simply too many opportunities to save money and avoid penalties, and too many complicated nuances relative to international taxation, for most people to manage this process themselves. Obviously there is also a point of diminishing returns—where the money paid to so many tax professionals outweighs the money that they can help the investor save—so the investor should consider the appropriate balance carefully. Generally speaking, however, a wealthy family has far more opportunities to save money and avoid penalties than the cost of enlisting qualified tax guidance on both sides of the border.

For both US and foreign-based tax counsel and accounting professionals (as well as immigration attorneys and service providers), I highly recommend a book entitled *Immigration Options for Investors and Entrepreneurs*, compiled by attorneys with a diverse set of backgrounds and skills. It contains an article entitled "Tax Implications of and Planning for Immigrant and Nonimmigrant Visas" by Albert and Miriam Golbert that provides outstanding coverage of this subject matter. The book, which was produced by the American Immigration Lawyers Association (AILA), can be purchased on Amazon.com through the following truncated url: tinyurl.com/dxetubq.

The total time actually spent in one country or another and the income earned in each country may have profound tax consequences. The United States and other countries typically tax their residents on worldwide income. There are severe consequences for failing to report income in a given country—even if that money was earned abroad and there was little likelihood of the taxing country discovering it. The more time a taxpayer spends in any given country, and the more income the individual is believed to have earned in that country, the greater claim the presiding tax authority has to taxes on that income. (Taxes on income earned at home are generally higher than taxes on income earned abroad, because it is believed that the government at home has provided more services and infrastructure support for which payment must be recovered.) Therefore, if taxpayers spend an equal or nearly equal amount of time residing in two or more countries, they will likely face higher tax liability than if they reside predominantly in one place, earning extra income abroad.

A professional tax adviser or tax attorney must spend many billable hours sorting out these convoluted messes and ensuring that no tax jurisdiction's toes have been stepped on. This adds even more cost and penalty to the beleaguered multinational taxpayer—to say nothing of the dramatically increased likelihood of audits and legal action and *those* associated, skyrocketing costs.

Dual residency does not comport with the spirit of the EB-5 Immigrant Investor Program or the tax laws of most countries, so both the reality and the appearance of such should be avoided.

Now that we have only the most superficial understanding of immigration tax law, we'll move on to chapter 8, which describes the process US businesses and entrepreneurs undergo to become eligible to attract immigrant investment.

CHAPTER 8

The Process for Companies: How Does a US Business Qualify to Attract EB-5 Investment?

US communities, companies, and development projects interested in funding their endeavors through EB-5 investment can be divided into two types: regional-center-level projects and direct EB-5 opportunities. What generally determines which one a company or project will choose are the number of direct jobs that are likely to result from the investment and the amount of investment required for the project. This chapter will analyze the two types of investment and discuss the steps that enterprises undertake to qualify as immigrant investment opportunities.

From the investor's perspective, it is important to recognize the steps that US enterprises must take, as this will allow the investor to ensure that the right elements are in place before subscribing to a particular investment.

Regional-Center-Level Projects

Generally speaking, communities, companies, and developers who wish to attract more than US$5 million will opt to either obtain an approved EB-5 regional center of their own or attempt to partner with a regional center that has already been approved. Projects that require at least US$5 million will most likely be trying to attract ten or more investors, which will precipitate the need for at least a hundred permanent full-time jobs. That many direct jobs are difficult to create and sustain with only US$5 million, so unless a significant amount of coinvestment by non-EB-5 investors is present, the project will need the benefit of indirect and induced jobs to satisfy the employment requirements of EB-5.

Communities, companies, and developers who want to obtain regional-center approval begin the arduous process with an I-924 Application for Regional Center Under the Immigrant Investor Pilot Program, which also requires a US$6,230 filing fee. Regional-center applicants submit their application, a business plan for the proposed regional center, a business plan and economic model for the first EB-5 project, and assorted legal and investment offering documents to USCIS and endure a four- to nine-month RFE and adjudication process.

I cut my teeth on the EB-5 program by authoring and submitting the first regional center approved in the state of Idaho back in 2009. That application—which was approved before either a filing fee or an actual application form existed—included approximately 325 pages comprised of the regional-center business plan, a project business plan for a statewide intellectual-property clearinghouse and investment fund, a comprehensive regionalized economic model for that project, and all of the associated legal and offering documents. The application also included maps and designations relative to Idaho's MSAs and TEAs, government and community support and partnership agreement letters, and letters of intent/memoranda of understanding from commercial and university partners. The full application took approximately six months to construct. The application drew two RFEs from

USCIS totaling twelve questions, and the total approval process was almost exactly six months.

By contrast, Idaho's second approved regional center—for gold mining and resort real estate—was submitted by an EB-5 experienced attorney who prepared an application (which I consulted on minimally) totaling more than 1,200 pages. That application received zero RFEs and was approved in early 2010 after exactly two months. These contrasting experiences underscore the value of working with experienced professionals. I count myself and my company among them now, but I was inexperienced at that time.

On the other hand, Idaho has had two more regional-center applicants since that time—both of which sought help and advice from some of the EB-5 industry's leading experts, and neither of which has received approval.

A regional-center approval is quite an achievement, but it is like getting your learner's permit. It is much more of a beginning than an end, because once they have gained approval, the owners/managers of the regional center must position it to successfully market to foreign investors, attract investment, and then successfully process the investors. A regional center that is unable to attract and process investment is worth only what it cost to gain approval.

Therefore, principals or communities that invest to obtain a regional center must not only have a plan for how to market and manage the regional center from an investor perspective, they must have sufficiently deep pockets to do so. I conservatively estimate that a regional center (which costs a total of between US$100,000 and US$150,000 to get approved, depending on how much work the applicants can do themselves) should have a minimum budget of US$500,000 per year set aside to set up, staff, and operate a regional center, and another US$500,000 to US$1 million per year to market the regional center abroad. Some of that money can be derived from income the regional center generates in administrative fees, and perhaps commission payments and licensing fees from projects, but it is very doubtful that the regional center can bring in enough income in its infancy to offset all of its costs. Therefore, I recommend a minimum bankroll of US$1.5 million to get a regional center through the full subscription of its first project. The real number is probably closer to US$2.5 million if the regional center hopes to fully fund its first project in less than one year.

Marketing comprises the lion's share of the expenses a regional center faces, particularly in the largest overseas EB-5 market, China. Overseas travel, lodging, event management, and channel partners' incentives and commissions account for the bulk of the expense, along with professionally produced and translated marketing materials. There are opportunities to drive costs down over time; however, a new regional center usually does not have the luxury of time or the experience to recognize cost-cutting measures that will not negatively impact results.

Direct EB-5 Commercial Enterprises

Generally, if a US company is looking to attract EB-5 investment in amounts less than US$5 million, then direct EB-5 is the way to go. The new jobs the company creates will all need to be direct employees of the company, so the fewer investors a company can attract the better. Also keep in mind that a small business attracting direct investors is most likely going to attract interest from people who understand the industry and are possibly looking to make a significant return on their investment. Therefore, they may also be willing to invest more than the minimum US$500,000—even in a rural area or TEA. When this occurs, it provides a major advantage to the private company, because it will have more money to create and sustain employment, and at the same time, it will require fewer investors and therefore be required to create fewer jobs. For example, four Korean EB-5 investors pooled their four US$1 million investments together to build an ethanol plant in South Dakota in the 1990s. I can't comment on the wisdom of their investment choice—or even if the company was successful—but it should not have been hard for them to achieve forty direct employees at the plant with US$4 million. In spite of oil price fluctuations, they may have obtained their unconditional residency and eventually naturalized as citizens.

Hopeful direct EB-5 companies must formulate and draft a comprehensive business plan and financial statements. They must also develop the necessary legal and offering documents that would be typical of an exempt small business (Securities Act Regulation D) offering—to include language warning the investors that they can have no guarantee of reimbursement and no access to their invested principal for at least two years.

The business plan, financial statements, and signed offering documents are submitted to USCIS along with the investor's I-526 petition and his or her evidentiary support documents. USCIS adjudicates the petition and renders a decision on the eligibility of the investment and the investor at the same time. Approval generally takes a little longer than investments through a regional center, likely between six and nine months.

In this chapter, we have identified the qualifying steps and criteria for US commercial enterprises relative to immigrant investment. In the next chapter, we will examine one additional investment-visa program that may provide expanded opportunity for various investors seeking US residency.

CHAPTER 9

Another US Investment-Visa Program: What if We Can't Quite Afford EB-5?

Some countries (as shown in Table D-1 in Appendix D) have forged trade and/or investment treaties with the United States. Citizens of these countries may be eligible for nonimmigrant (temporary/renewable) visas to manage their business affairs or investments in the United States. In this chapter, we will identify the two trade-treaty visas, and then closely examine the E-2 Treaty Investor visa.

E-1 visas are for business managers in treaty countries who must travel to and from the United States regularly to conduct trade of more than 50 percent of their company's total foreign trade volume. E-2 visas are for citizens of a treaty nation who invest in either a US-based business or a new US division or office of a foreign company, and who must travel regularly to and from the United States to manage the affairs of the US business or office. Some foreign countries have trade treaties, others have investment treaties, and some have both. Many countries—even several that you would not expect—have no trade or investment treaties with the United States at all (India for example).

E visas do not confer permanent residency, and they must be renewed after some predetermined period—sometimes annually or biannually. They are temporary, nonimmigrant visas. They do, however, permit the holder to obtain a social security number and a driver's license, and to earn income, open bank accounts, and purchase property in the United States. Like EB-5 visas, E visa petitions (the I-129 Petition for a Nonimmigrant Worker) can include the spouse and unmarried children less than twenty-one years of age. E-2 visas have a significantly lower minimum investment threshold than EB-5 immigrant visas. While there is not a set threshold, it has historically been between US$150,000 and US$200,000—the regulation simply says, "not a nominal investment." Renewal of an E visa requires verification of continued trade or investment and sustained operation in the approved business activity.

The E-1 and E-2 visa categories also permit employees of the approved business to petition for entry into the United States. The employee must have demonstrably unique skills or educational background, or must manage in an executive capacity.

Under certain circumstances, an E-2 investor visa can be "upgraded" to an EB-5 visa once the appropriate minimum investment threshold for EB-5 has been achieved.

Other advantages of the E-2 treaty-investor visa are that there is no residency requirement, and there is less likelihood of double taxation. E-2 visa holders may travel freely between the United States and their home country without a specific time requirement for presence in the United States. While an E-2 will be taxed by the United States on income earned in the United States, since they are not US residents, they may not be required to report worldwide income. Therefore, income earned in their home country may only be taxed by that country. The home country may also tax the income earned in the United States, but most countries provide either a deduction or a credit for taxes paid to foreign governments against income earned abroad. Once again, *consult a licensed tax professional with international tax-law experience.*

E visas complicate the immigrant investment process significantly, and they should be used very cautiously after careful analysis of the investor's qualifications and circumstances. However, under the right conditions, an E-2 visa may be the first step needed to an eventual EB-5 petition.

In the next chapter, we'll look over the landscape of the immigrant investment industry and learn to identify service providers who can help navigate it.

CHAPTER 10

A Shortage of Service Providers: How Do We Find Help If We Need It?

In this chapter, we will discuss the immigrant-investment service-provider market and provide some guidance in identifying and selecting qualified assistance. Since 2007, the number of approved EB-5 regional centers has expanded by more than 1,000 percent! Yet there are virtually the same numbers of experienced EB-5 service providers—particularly attorneys—as there were in 2007. This scarcity has been great for the few service providers who could jack up their prices based on the demand for their services, but it has been bad for investors and for companies and projects who hope to attract them. Even approved regional centers face difficulty in identifying and enlisting service providers with experience in any aspect of the EB-5 process—whether it be preparing or amending their projects, writing their economic models, processing their investors, or marketing their opportunities in foreign markets.

Inevitably, companies and investors will take a chance on inexperienced service providers—hopefully based on at least some general immigration or marketing experience they have. Some of those service providers will do a good job and be successful, and over time, the number of experienced service providers will grow.

Unfortunately in the meantime, many investors and companies will be victimized by this process.

To the extent that you don't have the capacity to absorb a big mistake or a total failure by a "wannabe" or neophyte EB-5 service provider, I recommend the following identification and evaluation process.

Look for Conflicts of Interest

Investors who contract with a service provider who works for an investment opportunity or assisted its owners should be cautioned that conflicts of interest may exist.

A conflict of interest exists when a service provider (such as an attorney, a consultant, or an investment adviser) is working for two entities at the same time and deriving income from both parties; or—if working for only one client—the interests of the service provider can potentially be placed ahead of the interests of the client.

Attorneys and investment advisers have a fiduciary responsibility to their clients. This means they must place the financial interests of their client ahead of their own interests and ahead of the interests of any other party to an agreement. In this way, the client is assured of getting the best possible advice and service from their service provider, and can be confident that the service provider is acting in the client's best interests.

When a conflict of interest arises, service providers who are fulfilling their fiduciary responsibility to their client must disclose the conflict. If the conflict of interest exists between the service provider and the client, then the client has the option of acknowledging and waiving the conflict of interest, resolving the conflict in some way, requesting that the service provider withdraw from the condition creating the conflict, or dissolving the service provider/client relationship.

When a conflict exists because of a condition in which a service provider is serving two interrelated clients, *both* clients must be made aware of the conflict and agree to waive it in order for the service provider to continue serving both clients.

I share all of this because when there are a limited number of skilled and experienced service providers available in a given industry or market, conflicts are bound to arise, and clients may not have the luxury or the desire to drop a service provider and simply go find another one. Consider, for example, an immigration attorney who works for both a foreign EB-5 investor and a US regional center. A conflict of interest exists because although the attorney has a fiduciary responsibility to his client the investor, he may in fact be getting the bulk of his pay from the regional center. If the attorney keeps the dual relationship secret, then he would indeed be guilty of an ethical violation and perhaps several law infractions. If a hardline ethical approach is taken, however, either the investor or the regional center could be faced with an inability to find qualified assistance. So while it is definitely the attorney's responsibility to *both* clients to disclose the conflict, it may be in the clients' best interest for both to acknowledge the conflict and to waive it.

Some would argue that the service-provider attorney cannot possibly act in the best interest of the client if he continues to process the investor's investment and immigration paperwork for what may not be the best or most appropriate regional-center investment opportunity for his client—especially if the marginal regional center is paying the attorney. They would also argue that the attorney is violating his fiduciary responsibility to the investor if he doesn't discourage him or her from that investment. Similarly, the attorney would be violating his fiduciary responsibility to the regional center if he discovers that the investor is somehow unqualified to make the investment and continues to process the transaction anyway.

However, as long as both clients are aware of the conflict of interest and agree to waive it—presumably because they trust the expert attorney not to misguide them—then both clients may avoid the hassle of having to compete in a scarce market for qualified service providers. Without question or limitation, however, if a service provider fails to disclose a known conflict of interest, or continues to work under the condition of a conflict against the wishes of any client, the provider is unethical and has likely violated the law. A client must always be afforded the opportunity to avoid a conflict of interest, and to choose an autonomous service provider.

In some cases or in some jurisdictions, it may be inappropriate or illegal for an attorney to accept payment—such as finder's fees—from an investee to whom he is referring clients. In such a situation, merely disclosing a conflict of interest will not absolve the attorney from legal responsibility for accepting such a payment.[20]

Before You Call—Study the Body of Work

If you have urgency or time constraints that preclude you from taking a chance on inexperienced help, then chances are you will be willing to pay a pretty high fee for a top-quality attorney or other service provider. You may also have to wait a little while for your chosen provider to be available to serve you, but not nearly as long as you will have to wait if a less-experienced service provider makes a mistake.

In this case, it is still important for you to investigate the service provider/firm and determine the true level of investment-visa experience. The service provider's website is a good starting point, but you should also check the websites of state bar associations and EB-5 service organizations for information about the service provider.

A website posting that says something to the effect of, "We have processed hundreds of EB-5 clients" or even, "*successfully* processed hundreds" does not mean that a service provider has necessarily led investors all the way through the process. The service provider making these claims may have simply submitted I-526 petitions for clients. If a service provider has successfully achieved unconditional resident status for clients, then that provider should show—or be willing to provide—redacted copies of USCIS approval letters (approval letters that have the private information of their clients blackened out) for both I-526 and I-829 petitions. Ask to see them.

Watch Out for the Wrong Type of Experience

Occasionally, I have found extremely knowledgeable experts who have vast academic understanding of the EB-5 program but, when a problem arises, lack the experience of being down in the weeds, fixing something that is broken—primarily because they have never actually completed or submitted an actual petition.

Similarly, an experienced immigration attorney, for example, who processes dozens of EB-5 visa petitions may not know the first thing about preparing, analyzing, or evaluating a business plan. Attorneys can bear significant malpractice liability for providing advice in areas in which they lack competence. Most of the time, these professionals will admit to having a deficit in some area, advise the client to seek specialty assistance, and possibly recommend another service provider. However, if you hire the service provider because of expertise in a certain area, don't be shocked when they don't have any experience at all in another more specific area. [21]

A framer and a finish carpenter both work on a house, and

perhaps they should be able to perform all aspects of the carpentry profession, but if you put them into a position to have to do both jobs, don't be surprised if you end up with a really funky-looking house! Specialization definitely exists in the immigration and investment professions as well.

I know an immigration attorney working in Taiwan who is an absolute whiz at completing and successfully processing I-526 visa petitions. It did not take long, however, to discover that he had virtually no understanding or expertise when it came to preparing or submitting a regional-center application, or even some of the basic rules to which regional centers must adhere. It was my mistake for thinking that one area of EB-5 expertise necessarily translated into all areas of EB-5.

Ask the Important Questions

If you don't ask about a service provider's true level of experience, you really don't know what you're going to get. If you do ask, the provider may still lie, but at least you've given an ethical person an opportunity to disclose any lack of experience. I have been in several meetings with attorneys who were held out to me by other people as having significant experience with EB-5. I always ask them, "Have you ever fully processed an I-829 petition?" If they say no or ask, "What's an I-829 Petition?" then I have my answer and I move on to the next question. If they say yes and I have never heard of this person before, I'm a little suspicious because there are still relatively few people who have done this, but I'll give them the benefit of the doubt in most cases because luckily, I have never had a person answer yes to one of these questions who later turned out to be lying. There have been plenty of times, however, that if I didn't ask the questions, I would never be told the answers—so *ask the questions.*

- "Have you ever had an EB-5 client awarded a conditional permanent resident visa?"
- "Have you ever had a visa application denied?" This is important because working through a denial can be a more powerful learning experience than an approval, and if they're embarrassed or evasive about their denials, this shows inexperience. If all they've ever had is denials, then that's another problem.
- "How long have you worked with the EB-5 program?" "How many I-526 approvals have you had?" "How many denials?" If they've truly had zero denials because they do such a good job, then that's fine, but chances are it is also because they haven't processed very many. Denials are not only the fault of the attorney/service provider, so over an extended number of applications, they are bound to get a denial.
- "Have you done any work with any other investment-visa programs?"
- "Do you currently work for any regional centers or companies seeking EB-5 investment?" "Would there be any conflicts of interest if you represented me as an investor?"
- "How much do you charge for this service?" If they have a definite answer to this question, they've probably done it before. If they say something like, "I'll have to check on that and get back to you," then chances are they don't have a clue how much work is entailed and they need to do some research.
- "Am I paying for a single, one-time service, or for a full two-year EB-5 process?"
- "What rights are guaranteed to me by the third

amendment to the US Constitution?" (I like to throw that one in to catch them off-guard!)

Know What Is Included for Your Payment

Like the administrative fee for the investment opportunity, you will want to thoroughly understand what services and indirect fees may be included by your service provider for the agreed-upon fee. An attorney who is paid to produce a petition for you may not include the USCIS processing fee for that petition, or even any follow-up with USCIS. Learn these details in advance.

Understand any guarantees that are made and the refund policy of the service provider. As is true with your administrative fee paid to the investment opportunity, you may forfeit some or all of your fee payment if a petition or investment is rejected through some fault of your own or as a result of false information that you supply.

Don't Overpay Less-Experienced Help

Because of the scarcity of experienced EB-5 professionals, you may be forced to work with someone who lacks specific EB-5 experience. In this case, be sure that the service provider has at least worked in other areas or industries that would provide skills and experience that relate to the EB-5 program. An immigration attorney or even a seasoned paralegal who has worked in an employment-based category (primarily H, L, and E, but also O, P, R, and TN) will not have difficulty understanding the technical requirements or USCIS processes of the EB-5 program, for example. Similarly, a licensed investment adviser or a licensed broker-dealer may have direct experience that relates to business-plan or investment analysis.

A full-service EB-5 consulting firm may employ or partner with several of these types of professionals as well as banking and real-estate professionals who don't have extensive EB-5-specific experience, but can add value to your EB-5 endeavor in other ways.

Don't pay someone to learn how to do EB-5. While some may need to learn as they go and charge you appropriately for their time, you should not pay high-priced attorneys an hourly rate while they read books and figure out if they can do this. It's fair for them to charge billable hours for the work that they actually perform on your behalf, but you shouldn't foot the bill for their education. Settle on a price for the whole job, and satisfy yourself that you're not getting worked over for hours the attorney or other service provider is going to spend reading and surfing the Internet looking for clues.

A very respectable and professional attorney I know in Idaho had virtually no experience with EB-5 or even with immigration. When he was asked if he could help a community with their regional-center application, he told them, "I don't have any experience with this, but I'm willing to learn, and I won't charge you nearly as much as if I knew what I was doing." Today he and his firm have the experience, and he can charge as much as he wants. If you have to work with an inexperienced attorney, that's the kind you want.

CHAPTER 11

Conclusions: What Do We Do First?

Certain Security has been intentionally positioned as a consumer's guide to US investment-visa programs. I hope it has provided you with enough detailed information in an understandable format to help you and encourage you in making an immigrant investment decision for your family. Perhaps after reading the book, however, you have even less *certainty* about these programs and about your decision than before. I cannot overemphasize how important it is for you to seek additional information and assistance to overcome any trepidation that you may have. There are knowledgeable, experienced people who can assist you in getting your family to a secure life in the United States.

My company, Inversión Consultant Services, is well-qualified to provide you with any assistance you may need, and for any service we may not be qualified to offer—such as tax advice—we have excellent relationships with professionals who *are* qualified. We would be pleased to assist you with any aspect of the immigrant investment process. Visit our website at icsinusa.com for contact information.

It is also quite possible that, after reading this book, you have determined that you can manage this process yourself. I don't blame you. I managed the immigration process for members of my own family without hiring any lawyers, and I have assisted many other investors with various steps of the process without the need for legal or other professional assistance. It can be done. Nevertheless, immigrant investment (which adheres to unknown or ambiguous rules and regulations), investment analysis and selection, and tax, securities, and corporate law are complicated business even for people with a strong command of the English language. I can't recommend more strongly that any interested investors seek the advice and assistance of trained professionals. They will be most valuable in avoiding mistakes—which cost an enormous amount of time and money to correct—and in cleaning up messes that inevitably get made in such a complex process. The time and money you save may be exponentially more valuable than the time and money you spend to get the right help for the job.

So what should you do first? You may want to take a good look at your specific qualifications for investment-visa programs, but having verified your eligibility, start with Step 1 in chapter 5—"Prepare"—and get going on your written plan and gathering your documents. Then start contacting potential service providers for the parts of the process you are not comfortable handling alone. I encourage you to visit familysecuritynow.com, icsinusa.com, and blog.icsinusa.com for additional information and assistance and for regular updates on investment-visa programs. At familysecuritynow.com, you can get access to a training system I developed—the Certain Security Investment-Visa Success System—that guides investors and their families step-by-step through the entire immigrant investment process.

If you're a Spanish speaker, our Spanish sites are SeguridadFamilia.com.mx, icsinusa.com.mx, and invertir.icsinusa.com.mx. You can find Spanish translations of most of our materials at those sites. *Certain Security* will be available in Spanish in early 2013 under the title *Seguridad Familiar*. Our Spanish Facebook site is facebook.com/icsmex and we are @ICSMEX on Twitter.

We hope to be releasing our materials—including our books—in many other languages and countries in the coming months. Monitor blog.icsinusa.com and FamilySecurityNow.com regularly for news about upcoming release dates, and you can also visit our company pages on Facebook (facebook.com/icsinusa and facebook.com/famsecure) and watch for regular Tweets on Twitter (@ICSinUSA and @FamSecure). Naturally, I encourage you to "like" us and "follow" us. More social-media presence will be developed shortly with Google+, LinkedIn, Tumblr, and YouTube.

The most important step for you, though, is *start*. Don't wait until tragedy strikes to take action and secure the future of your family and your children. Inversión Consultant Services and my family and I offer you and your family best wishes for continued safety and prosperity.

Appendices

APPENDIX A

EB-5 Checklists

Company Relocation/Expansion Direct
EB-5 Investment Checklist

The following checklist identifies and prioritizes the steps to relocating or expanding an existing foreign business as an eligible direct EB-5 immigrant investment. When applicable, a projected cost is presented that can reasonably be expected for that step if contracting for specific services.

- ☐ Develop a comprehensive written plan and timeline for the investment and company/family relocation processes.
- ☐ Begin to gather supporting documentation for the investment-visa petition.
- ☐ Determine the appropriateness/eligibility of the proposed relocation/expansion project for EB-5 purposes.
- ☐ Choose a US site for the project that is within either a Targeted Employment Area (TEA) or a rural area as defined by USCIS.
- ☐ Identify service providers and execute appropriate

contracts for services. Pay retainers and/or initial installment on administrative fee (approx. US$50,000).
- ☐ Register US business enterprise (sole proprietorship, partnership, limited liability company, or corporation) in the jurisdiction of the chosen site (US$250).
- ☐ Secure US Taxpayer Identification (Employer Identification) number for the new business enterprise (US$50).
- ☐ Open US bank accounts for the new commercial enterprise, and deposit at least US$500,000 (plus wire transfer fees as applicable).
- ☐ If necessary, apply to state-authorized authority for TEA analysis/designation (US$300).
- ☐ Determine the number of direct permanent full-time jobs that will be created by the project.
- ☐ Determine the total amount and use of all invested funds in the project.
- ☐ Write a comprehensive business plan for the project—tailoring various elements of the plan to the EB-5 Immigrant Investor Program (US$5,000 to US$10,000).
- ☐ Develop pro forma financial statements for the project—also tailored to the EB-5 program (US$500 to US$1,000).
- ☐ Develop assorted legal documents for the EB-5 investment as defined by USCIS—including operating agreement and accredited investor checklist (US$10,000 to US$15,000).
- ☐ Assemble and translate supporting immigration and financial documentation of investors and dependents, including background checks, source of funds due

diligence, and birth and marriage records (US$10,000 per investor).
- ☐ Submit I-526 petition and other USCIS applications as necessary and perform necessary follow-up to requests for evidence (US$7,000 to US$10,000 including USCIS administrative fees).
- ☐ Upon I-526 approval, schedule and attend US State Department consular interview for receipt of conditional permanent resident visa.
- ☐ Operate and manage commercial enterprise over the next two and a half years, ensuring the employment of at least ten full-time authorized US workers—not counting any of the investor's immediate family.
- ☐ Assemble and submit I-829 Petition by Entrepreneur to Remove Conditions, verifying that the invested funds remained at risk for the two-year investment period and that ten full-time employees are employed as of the date of the I-829 application (US$5,000 including USCIS administrative fees).
- ☐ Upon approval of the I-829 petition, receive unconditional permanent resident US visa.
- ☐ After five years from the date of I-526 approval, apply for naturalized citizenship status if desired.

Direct EB-5 Investment Checklist

The following checklist identifies and prioritizes the steps for making a direct EB-5 immigrant investment into an existing or new US business.

- ☐ Develop a comprehensive written plan for the investment, immigration, and family relocation processes.

- ☐ Begin to gather supporting documentation for investment-visa petition.
- ☐ Identify service providers and execute appropriate contracts for services. Pay retainers and/or initial installments on service fees.
- ☐ Identify, analyze, and select an EB-5-eligible direct-investment opportunity.
- ☐ Assemble and translate supporting immigration and financial documentation of investors and dependents including background checks, source of funds due diligence, and birth and marriage records.
- ☐ Complete the I-526 visa petition and compile and assemble all supporting evidentiary documentation.
- ☐ Sign associated subscription, private placement, operating, partnership, and escrow agreements as applicable.
- ☐ Invest at least US$500,000 in the chosen US commercial enterprise.
- ☐ Pay the applicable administrative fee.
- ☐ Submit I-526 visa petition to USCIS for approval, along with company's EB-5-specific business plan, financial statements, and legal documents.
- ☐ Respond to Requests for Evidence (RFEs) from USCIS.
- ☐ If desired, obtain a US visitor's visa (B-1 or B-2) and visit/investigate US communities where you and your family might like to reside. Identify service providers relative to family relocation (real estate, banking, education, etc.).
- ☐ Upon I-526 approval, schedule US Consulate interview.

- ☐ Upon award of the conditional permanent resident visa, begin family relocation process.
- ☐ Engage in managerial capacity with company receiving investment—closely monitoring capital deployment and job creation.
- ☐ Within ninety days of two-year anniversary of award of conditional visa, prepare and submit I-829 Petition by Entrepreneur to Remove Conditions.

EB-5 Regional-Center Investment Checklist

The following checklist identifies and prioritizes the steps to making a qualified investment in an EB-5 regional center.

- ☐ Develop a comprehensive written plan for the investment, immigration, and family-relocation processes.
- ☐ Begin to gather supporting documentation for investment-visa petition.
- ☐ Identify service providers and execute appropriate contracts for services. Pay retainers and/or initial installments on service fees.
- ☐ Identify, analyze, and select an approved EB-5 regional-center investment opportunity.
- ☐ Assemble and translate supporting immigration and financial documentation of investors and dependents including background checks, source of funds due diligence, and birth and marriage records.
- ☐ Complete the I-526 visa petition and compile and assemble all supporting evidentiary documentation.
- ☐ Sign associated subscription, Private Placement, operating, partnership, and escrow agreements as applicable.

- ☐ Invest at least US$500,000 in the chosen regional center.
- ☐ Pay the applicable administrative fee.
- ☐ Submit I-526 visa petition to USCIS for approval of your immigration petition, along with the regional center's I-797B notice of approval.
- ☐ Respond to RFEs from USCIS.
- ☐ If desired, obtain a US visitor's visa (B-1 or B-2) and visit/investigate US communities where you and your family might like to reside. Identify service providers relative to family relocation (real estate, banking, education).
- ☐ Upon I-526 approval, schedule US Consulate interview.
- ☐ Upon award of the conditional permanent resident visa, begin family-relocation process.
- ☐ Engage in managerial capacity with regional center receiving investment, closely monitoring capital deployment and job creation.
- ☐ Within ninety days of two-year anniversary of award of conditional visa, prepare and submit I-829 Petition by Entrepreneur to Remove Conditions with appropriate evidentiary support from the regional center.

APPENDIX B
I-526 Visa Petition Checklist

- [ ] A thorough and highly professional but concise cover letter that acts as an "executive summary" of the overall document
- [ ] Completed and signed I-526 Immigrant Petition for Alien Entrepreneur
- [ ] Birth, marriage, and adoption records and passports of investor, spouse, and all minor dependent children under age twenty-one at the time of I-526 submission
- [ ] Background investigation of all immediate family members as appropriate
- [ ] Credit report of investor and spouse
- [ ] Business and personal bank and tax records for past five years
- [ ] Documentary evidence of net worth and asset ownership
- [ ] G-28 Notice of Entry of Appearance as Attorney or Accredited Representative—naming the investor applicant's legal representative (if applicable)
- [ ] Filing fee of US$1,500

Specific Requirements for EB-5 Regional-Center Investors

- ☐ Copy of the regional-center approval letter
- ☐ Copy of the signed EB-5 investor subscription agreement
- ☐ Evidentiary document showing escrow of invested funds (US$500,000 or US$1 million)

Specific Requirements for Direct EB-5 Investors

- ☐ Copy of the commercial-enterprise business plan—including historical and pro forma financial statements
- ☐ Evidentiary proof of at-risk investment (US$500,000 or US$1 million)
- ☐ A copy of the signed subscription agreement, terms sheet, operating agreement, or other appropriate investment document
- ☐ Evidence of the investor's education and relevant knowledge or experience in the commercial enterprise's industry
- ☐ Optional support letters from US, state, and local government officials

For both regional-center and direct EB-5 investors who already have a nonimmigrant status, documentation of that status (i.e. copies of visas) should be submitted with the I-526.

APPENDIX C

EB-5 Investment Case Studies

The basis of investment in an EB-5 regional center is that many foreign investors are pooled together to invest in a larger project—usually between US$10 million and US$300 million. This means that between twenty and six hundred investors' funds will be managed together on the EB-5 project.

Regional-center investors enjoy the benefit of sharing the project's risk with many other EB-5 investors—and frequently, domestic US investors too—so that the success of the project is not dependent on only one or just a few EB-5 investors' funds. Regional-center investors also benefit from easier satisfaction of job-creation requirements, improving the likelihood that the conditions will be removed from their permanent resident visas, because regional centers count indirect and induced job creation in addition to direct jobs.

On the other hand, EB-5 investors who invest through a regional center are usually insulated from ownership and management of the EB-5 project through business models such as limited partnerships. This may severely limit the investors' managerial authority over their investment funds and the course of the business. Historically, regional centers have also offered only marginal returns on invested EB-5 capital.

Hypothetical Case Study No. 1: Direct EB-5 Investment in US Enterprise

"I don't have my own company, but I also want to keep a close eye on my investment. I don't feel 'in control' with a regional-center investment."

Because of the limitations of regional-center investments, many EB-5 investors choose to invest directly in a US commercial enterprise—either alone or with just a few other EB-5 investors. Direct EB-5 investors have the opportunity to be equity partners and to hold management positions in the US company and to more closely monitor the use of their investments.

Tomas Menendez was a forty-six-year-old barkeeper and nightclub owner in Saltillo, Mexico, and a married father of three beautiful children. He had concerns about the personal security of his family and was very interested in immigrating permanently to the United States—even though he was still interested in owning and managing his businesses in Saltillo. Tomas had taken a close look at some very compelling EB-5 regional-center investment opportunities in the United States, but the interest or returns that they were offering were just not very exciting. Having successfully grown and operated his own business, he felt certain he could do better managing a business in the United States himself. Unfortunately, his English-language skills were limited, and he didn't have a lot of confidence about having the same success in the nightclub business in the United States as he had enjoyed in Mexico. He wondered if perhaps he were to find and join with the right American partners, he might be able to make a qualifying EB-5 investment and help the US company become successful.

Tomas and his wife were introduced to two American men from Amarillo, Texas, who were planning to open a hacienda-style hotel and were looking for US$1 million in EB-5 investment from up to two investors. What interested Tomas about their project was that it included an upscale cantina cocktail lounge and nightclub. The Americans were very excited about Tomas's experience because they hadn't found anyone to run the club yet, and they had hoped to give the club a Latin ambience.

The American partners were offering 30 percent of the company's ownership to the EB-5 investors, and the projected profits were very attractive to Tomas—particularly since he would be managing part of the business and have a direct hand in its success. Even though Tomas had been planning on investing only US$500,000 through the EB-5 program, he decided to capture the entire 30 percent share of the company for himself and invested US$1 million. This meant that the company would only be required to produce ten direct, full-time jobs for the EB-5 program instead of twenty. Tomas accepted the job as the hotel's food and beverage manager—in addition to his role as a voting, 30 percent partner in the company.

In Amarillo, Tomas and his family found a vibrant Hispanic community, outstanding public and private schools, excellent English as a Second Language programs for Tomas and his wife, and several safe and affordable residential neighborhoods. USCIS was impressed by the expertise that Tomas brought to the company from his business background in Mexico. The Menendez family's conditional permanent resident visas were approved and issued in approximately four months.

Hypothetical Case Study No. 2: EB-5 Regional-Center Investment

"I really don't care how you manage my money, as long as I get it back and I get the visas for my family as quickly and smoothly as possible."

Frequently, EB-5 investors have reservations about starting or managing a business of their own in the United States, and they also worry about the risk of investing in a small business that someone else owns. At the same time, they are concerned about a small business's ability to create the necessary direct employment required for direct EB-5 investment. For these families, the EB-5 regional center is an attractive option.

Regina Velazquez was thirty-eight years old when her husband was killed in an automobile accident in their home city of Guadalajara. Mr. Velazquez left Regina with two young sons, and although the family was devastated by his loss, the life-insurance settlement, together with the young couple's trust funds, sufficiently provided for Regina and the children's financial security.

Unfortunately, news of Mr. Velazquez's accident and the subsequent financial outcomes for Regina and her boys were widely publicized in the Guadalajara press, and before long, some unsavory characters began to come around the Velazquez home. Regina still felt safe in her home and neighborhood, but she began to worry about what dangers there might be for her and her sons whenever they moved about the city.

A friend told Regina about the EB-5 Immigrant Investor Program. Her friend and her friend's husband had invested in an EB-5 regional center in San Diego, California, and were living comfortably there with their family. Regina had always thought of sending her sons abroad for their education, and she was still young herself, so the thought of immigrating to the United States seemed romantic and intriguing to her. The regional-center program was very attractive to Regina because she didn't own a business, and frankly, she didn't know the first thing about investing or managing a business. The limited influence and responsibility of a voting board of directors' position seemed just right for her based on her lack of business experience.

Regina wanted to get out of Guadalajara quickly, though, and she wondered how long the process would take. The regional center that she chose had a successful five-year track record of quickly and efficiently processing immigration applications.

The regional-center investment also increased the likelihood that the conditions would be removed from Regina and her sons' visas, because the regional center had the benefit of counting indirect and induced job creation. Not only would direct employees of the project company be counted, but indirect employees like those hired by the company's suppliers and subcontractors, and induced employees like those hired by the new fast-food restaurant across the street would all count toward the EB-5 investors' job creation requirements. This made tremendous sense to Regina.

She made an investment of US$500,000 in the regional center—which was building senior assisted-living facilities in Arizona—and paid US$65,000 in administrative fees to cover the costs of all of her family's immigration processing for the full two and a half years of her investment. The administrative fees also included legal representation, banking fees, and housing location assistance for Regina. She and her sons purchased and moved into a comfortable home near Santa Barbara, California.

Hypothetical Case Study No. 3: EB-5 Investment for Adult Children

"I don't really want to immigrate or live full-time in the United States. Can my adult son or daughter make the investment instead?"

Obtaining an immigrant or nonimmigrant investment visa with adult children presents a unique situation. Only unmarried children under the age of twenty-one can be included on parents' visa petitions. Therefore, if foreign citizens hope to have their adult children accompany them to the United States, or if the adult children are to immigrate separately, then the children will have to apply for visas under different programs.

At the same time, more mature parents are often discouraged

by the requirement that they will have to spend a minimum of six months of each year in the United States in order to satisfy the visa requirements for permanent residence. They are also frequently frustrated by the likelihood of double taxation, as they intend to spend significant portions of their time in both the United States and their home country.

A solution to this dilemma is for the parents to "gift" investment funds to their adult children so that *they* may immigrate to the United States for various reasons.

Ernesto Alvarado was a fifty-eight-year-old successful owner of a textile-export business based in Veracruz. He had built a very large business and considerable wealth by exporting clothing and other textile products to the United States and other countries. He had always seriously considered opening a distribution facility in Texas or California, and he was attracted to the idea of immigrating to the United States, but the fact was, Ernesto was afraid of such a big change at his age—and more importantly, he couldn't envision a time when his very large manufacturing and export operations in Veracruz could manage six months or more of operating without his direct supervision.

But now, Ernesto's oldest daughter, Maria, age twenty-six, had obtained her MBA from a university in Mexico City, and she had been managing the company's export distribution for the past three years. He also had a son Miguel, age twenty-one, who was about to graduate from a prestigious technical university, and Miguel wanted to study engineering in the United States. To add fear and urgency to Ernesto's situation, Maria had been the victim of a failed kidnapping attempt the year before.

Ernesto learned that the EB-5 Immigrant Investor Program could be used to move his adult children to the United States, and that investing in the expansion of his company there would qualify as a direct EB-5 investment—as long as the investment dollars remained at risk for two years, and each investment of US$500,000 or more resulted in ten permanent full-time US employees.

Ernesto decided to gift each of his adult children US$600,000, which they invested in the establishment of a US distribution facility in a Targeted Employment Area near Pascagoula, Mississippi. They used some of the money to pay their administrative fees, and had some money left with which to find a home and get settled. Ernesto chose Mississippi because of the inexpensive real estate and the fact that he could accompany a container shipment out of Veracruz and visit his children from time to time.

Maria became the chief executive officer of the new US limited-liability company that they created, and Miguel participated as a voting member of the company so that he could concentrate on his engineering studies at the University of Mississippi.

They purchased a house near the beach in Biloxi, Mississippi, where Maria lives, which entitled Miguel to state resident tuition at the university.

Ernesto and his wife, Carmen, visited Maria and Miguel regularly over the next several years. They noticed how much more peaceful and safe Mississippi was and how comfortable they felt whenever they visited. Five years after their EB-5 investment—and when Ernesto was ready to retire from his career in textiles—Maria became a naturalized US citizen and sponsored her parents on permanent resident visas. Today, they split their time between Mississippi and Veracruz, where much of their family still resides. Their old house in Veracruz has now become their vacation home.

APPENDIX D

Trade and Investment Treaty Nations

Table D-1: E-1 and E-2 Trade and Investment Treaty Nations[22]

Country	E-Visa
Albania	E-2
Argentina	E-1
Argentina	E-2
Armenia	E-2
Australia	E-1
Australia	E-2
Austria	E-1
Austria	E-2
Azerbaijan	E-2
Bahrain	E-2
Bangladesh	E-2
Belgium	E-1
Belgium	E-2

Country	E-Visa
Bolivia	E-1
Bolivia	E-2
Bosnia and Herzegovina[1]	E-1
Bosnia and Herzegovina[1]	E-2
Brunei	E-1
Bulgaria	E-2
Cameroon	E-2
Canada	E-1
Canada	E-2
Chile	E-1
Chile	E-2
China (Taiwan)[2]	E-1
China (Taiwan)[2]	E-2

Country	E-Visa		Country	E-Visa
Colombia	E-1		Finland	E-2
Colombia	E-2		France[6]	E-1
Congo (Brazzaville)	E-2		France[6]	E-2
Congo (Kinshasa)	E-2		Georgia	E-2
Costa Rica	E-1		Germany	E-1
Costa Rica	E-2		Germany	E-2
Czech Republic[4]	E-2		Greece	E-1
Denmark[5]	E-1		Grenada	E-2
Denmark[5]	E-2		Honduras	E-1
Ecuador	E-2		Honduras	E-2
Egypt	E-2		Iran	E-1
Estonia	E-1		Iran	E-2
Estonia	E-2		Ireland	E-1
Croatia[3]	E-1		Ireland	E-2
Croatia[3]	E-2		Israel	E-1
Czech Republic[4]	E-2		Italy	E-1
Denmark[5]	E-1		Italy	E-2
Denmark[5]	E-2		Jamaica	E-2
Ecuador	E-2		Japan[7]	E-1
Egypt	E-2		Japan[7]	E-2
Estonia	E-1		Jordan	E-1
Estonia	E-2		Jordan	E-2
Ethiopia	E-1		Kazakhstan	E-2
Ethiopia	E-2		Korea (South)	E-1
Finland	E-1		Korea (South)	E-2

Country	E-Visa
Kosovo[8]	E-1
Kosovo[8]	E-2
Kyrgyzstan	E-2
Latvia	E-1
Latvia	E-2
Liberia	E-1
Liberia	E-2
Lithuania	E-2
Luxembourg	E-1
Luxembourg	E-2
Macedonia	E-1
Macedonia	E-2
Mexico	E-1
Mexico	E-2
Moldova	E-2
Mongolia	E-2
Montenegro[9]	E-1
Montenegro[9]	E-2
Morocco	E-2
Netherlands[10]	E-1
Netherlands[10]	E-2
Norway[11]	E-1
Norway[11]	E-2
Oman	E-1
Oman	E-2

Country	E-Visa
Pakistan	E-1
Pakistan	E-2
Panama	E-2
Paraguay	E-1
Paraguay	E-2
Philippines	E-1
Philippines	E-2
Poland	E-1
Poland	E-2
Romania	E-2
Serbia[12]	E-1
Serbia[12]	E-2
Senegal	E-2
Singapore	E-1
Singapore	E-2
Slovak Republic[13]	E-2
Slovenia[14]	E-1
Slovenia[14]	E-2
Spain[15]	E-1
Spain[15]	E-2
Sri Lanka	E-2
Suriname[16]	E-1
Suriname[16]	E-2
Sweden	E-1
Sweden	E-2

Country	E-Visa
Switzerland	E-1
Switzerland	E-2
Thailand	E-1
Thailand	E-2
Togo	E-1
Togo	E-2
Trinidad & Tobago	E-2
Tunisia	E-2
Turkey	E-1
Turkey	E-2
Ukraine	E-2
United Kingdom[17]	E-1
United Kingdom[17]	E-2
Yugoslavia[18]	E-1
Yugoslavia[18]	E-2

Country Specific Footnotes for Table D-1[23]

1. **Bosnia-Herzegovina**: The countries that made up the former Socialist Federal Republic of Yugoslavia (SFRY)—including Bosnia and Herzegovina, Croatia, the Former Yugoslav Republic of Macedonia, Slovenia, and the Federal Republic of Yugoslavia—continue to be bound by the treaty in force with the SFRY when it was dissolved.

2. **China (Taiwan)**: The trade and investment treaty signed with Taiwan prior to January 1, 1979, is administered by the American Institute in Taiwan—a Washington, DC, nonprofit corporation. The

agreement does not recognize Taiwan or its government and does not imply any official relationship between the United States and Taiwan.

3. **Croatia:** See Bosnia-Herzegovina.
4. **Czech Republic**: The investment-only treaty that was signed between the United States and the Czech and Slovak Federal Republic on December 19, 1992, was renewed on January 1, 1993, with the separate states of the Czech Republic and Slovak Republic.
5. **Denmark**: Greenland and its Danish citizens are not included in Denmark's July 30, 1961, treaty.
6. **France**: The treaty that entered into force on December 21, 1960, applies to the departments of Martinique, Guadeloupe, French Guiana, and Reunion.
7. **Japan**: The Bonin Islands and the Ryukyu Islands were subsequently added to the Japanese trade and investment agreement previously signed on October 30, 1953.
8. **Kosovo:** See Bosnia-Herzegovina.
9. **Montenegro:** See Bosnia-Herzegovina.
10. **Netherlands**: The treaty that entered into force on December 5, 1957, is applicable to Aruba and Netherlands Antilles.
11. **Norway**: Norway's September 13, 1932, treaty does not apply to Svalbard or any of its islands.
12. **Serbia**: See Bosnia-Herzegovina.
13. **Slovak Republic:** See Czech Republic.
14. **Slovenia:** See Bosnia-Herzegovina.
15. **Spain**: All Spanish territories are included in their trade and investment treaty signed April 14, 1903.
16. **Suriname**: The treaty with the Netherlands that

entered into force December 5, 1957, was made applicable to Suriname on February 10, 1963.

17. **United Kingdom**: On July 3, 1815, the United States signed a trade and investment treaty with United Kingdom countries and territories in Europe and people who "reside actually and permanently and have domicile there." This includes the British Isles, the Channel Islands, and Gibraltar. The Republic of Ireland is excluded. Qualification for trader or investor status under this treaty requires that the alien be a national of the United Kingdom. Foreign nationals of other commonwealth nations outside of Europe do not qualify for treaty trader or treaty investor status under the United Kingdom treaty.

18. **Yugoslavia:** See Bosnia-Herzegovina.

Glossary of Terms

I've really tried as hard as possible to avoid using legal or business jargon in this book and to clearly define all immigrant-investment terminology and acronyms within the text. Nevertheless, here is a list of definitions to further clarify any oversights or ambiguities.

Terminology

Accredited investor: an entity or natural person (in this case *only* a natural person) who has a net worth exceeding US$1 million exclusive of his or her primary residence *or* who has personal annual income of at least US$200,000 (or household income of US$300,000) for each of the previous two tax years and expects to earn at least that much in the current tax year. A person of such means would be deemed savvy enough about business and investing to assume the risk of an investment decision and also deemed to have the capacity to absorb a complete loss.

At-risk period: the two years immediately following the date of EB-5 investment during which the investor may not have access to or personal use of the invested principal or receive any reimbursement of that principal.

Business plan: a formal, comprehensive document explaining the nature, industry, markets, management, operation, and financial goals and strategies of a business or project.

E visa: the E series temporary (nonimmigrant) worker visa for citizens of trade or investment treaty nations. E-1 visas are for treaty traders and qualified employees, while E-2s are for treaty investors and employees.

Economic model: an economic-impact analysis prepared for a regional center by a professional regional economist who uses accepted formulas, statistical methodologies, and multipliers to forecast the employment of a given project and the economic impact on its region, based on the amount of investment applied to the project.

Metropolitan Statistical Area (MSA): a geographic region determined by the US Office of Management and Budget to have a high population density at its core and close economic ties throughout the area. Rural areas adjacent to a city, for example, may be absorbed into that city's MSA if the majority of workers from those areas commute into the city for employment.

Regional center: an EB-5 Immigrant Investment Regional Center as established by approval of USCIS and authorized to attract and pool multiple qualified EB-5 investors to fund the establishment and operation of commercial enterprises or development projects in the United States, designed to create direct, indirect, and induced jobs in sufficient numbers to satisfy the aggregate employment requirements of the regional center's investors.

Request for Evidence (RFE): any request by USCIS for additional information, clarification, or documentary proof relative to the adjudication of a visa petition or other application.

Rural area: an area that is both outside of any MSA *and* outside the boundary of any community with a population exceeding twenty thousand.

Targeted Employment Area (TEA): a geographic or geopolitical area that is either within an MSA *or* within the boundary of a community with a population exceeding twenty thousand that is experiencing unemployment exceeding 150 percent of the national average. A TEA may be defined by federal labor statistics that confirm its high unemployment condition, or it may be designated by a state government official selected by that state's governor.

United States Citizenship and Immigration Services (USCIS): the agency within the US Department of Homeland Security that administers US immigration policy, including investment-visa programs.

Acronyms

E-2: a temporary, renewable nonimmigrant US visa for foreign investors from countries governed by a US trade and/or investment treaty.

EB-5: an employment-based, fifth-preference program for permanent resident immigrant visas administered by US Citizenship and Immigration Services (USCIS) through which foreign citizens are awarded US residency in exchange for investment in a US commercial enterprise that results in permanent, full-time employment by US workers.

MSA: Metropolitan Statistical Area.

RFE: Request for Evidence.

TEA: Targeted Employment Area.

USCIS: United States Citizenship and Immigration Services.

USCIS Immigration Forms Pertaining to Investment Visa Programs

G-28: the form G-28 Notice of Entry of Appearance as Attorney or Accredited Representative used by an immigration applicant to identify and authorize an attorney or other representative who will communicate with USCIS on behalf of the petitioner and who may accompany the petitioner at an interview. The G-28I is used to appoint an international attorney to act on behalf of the petitioner outside the United States.

I-9: the form I-9 Employment Eligibility Verification used to verify a foreign citizen's authorization to work and to earn wages or salary in the United States. The I-9 may also be used in conjunction with the I-829 petition to verify the employment of sufficient workers to satisfy EB-5 requirements.

I-129: the form I-129 Petition for a Nonimmigrant Worker visa application submitted by an E-2 investor (among many others).

I-485: the form I-485 Application to Register Permanent Residence or Adjust Status used by a foreign citizen who already resides in the United States to change from one visa status to another—for example, from a temporary status to a permanent one.

I-526: the form I-526 Immigrant Petition for Alien Entrepreneur visa application submitted by an EB-5 immigrant investor.

I-797: the form I-797 Notice of Action. The I-797 with various sub-letters (I-797e, for example) is used by USCIS for receipt acknowledgments, approval and denial notices, and requests for evidence.

I-829: the form I-829 Petition by Entrepreneur to Remove Conditions submitted within ninety days of the second anniversary of the date on which a conditional visa was received. Approval of an I-829 petition signifies that all EB-5 requirements have been satisfied and that unconditional permanent residency has been awarded.

I-924: the form I-924 Application for Regional Center under the Immigrant Investor Pilot Program used by companies, communities, or development projects to apply for approval as an EB-5 Immigrant Investment Regional Center.

I-924A: the form I-924A Supplement to Form I-924 used by approved regional centers to amend elements of their approved application, to submit subsequent projects for approval, and to file their annual reports.

Bibliography

Arias, Elsie Hui, and Lincoln Stone. "Navigating the Lawful Source Requirement for EB-5 Immigration." In *Immigration Options for Investors and Entrepreneurs*, edited by Lincoln Stone et al. Washington, DC: American Immigration Lawyers Association, 2010.

Consejo para la Ley y los Derechos Humanos (The Council for the Law and Human Rights). "Expediente Ciudadano" (Special Report on Extortion). CLDH organizational website. March 1, 2013. http://mexicodenuncia.org/extorsion.html.

Golbert, Albert S., and Miriam J. Golbert. "Tax Implications of and Planning for Immigrant and Nonimmigrant Visas." In *Immigration Options for Investors and Entrepreneurs*, edited by Lincoln Stone et al. Washington, DC: American Immigration Lawyers Association, 2010.

Investopedia. "Dictionary." Economic/investment website. March 1, 2013. http://www.investopedia.com/dictionary/.

Joseph, Peter. *IIUSA* (blog), Association to Invest in USA. http://iiusablog.org.

Juceam, Robert E., Denyse Sabagh, and Roxana C. Bacon. "A Roundtable on Ethical Considerations and Professional Risks in Investment Immigration." In *Immigration Options for Investors and Entrepreneurs*, edited by Lincoln Stone et al. Washington, DC: American Immigration Lawyers Association, 2010.

OANDA. "Historical Exchange Rates." Foreign exchange currency trading website. 2012. http://www.oanda.com/currency/historical-rates/.

Organisation for Economic Co-operation and Development (OECD). "Tax Revenue as Percentage of GDP." OECD organizational website. 2012. http://stats.oecd.org/Index.aspx?DataSetCode=REV.

United States Bureau of Labor Statistics (BLS). "Consumer Price Indexes for All Urban Consumers (CPI-U)." Government website. 2012. http://www.bls.gov/ro3/fax_9125.pdf.

United States Citizenship and Immigration Services (USCIS). "EB-5 Immigrant Investor." Government website. 2012. http://www.uscis.gov/portal/site/uscis/menuitem. eb1d4c2 a3e5b9ac89243c6a7543f6d1a/?vgnextoid=facb8345 3d4a 3210VgnVCM100000b92ca60aRCRD&vgnextchannel=f acb83453d4a3210VgnVCM100000b92ca60aRCRD.

United States Citizenship and Immigration Services (USCIS). "EB-5 Immigrant Investor Program." Presentation at stakeholder meeting, September 15, 2011.

United States Citizenship and Immigration Services (USCIS). "Forms." Government website. March 1, 2013. http://www.uscis.gov/forms.

United States Citizenship and Immigration Services (USCIS). "Immigrant Investment Statistics." Reported at October 2012 quarterly EB-5 stakeholder meeting.

United States Citizenship and Immigration Services (USCIS). "Immigrant Investor Regional Centers." Government website. March 1, 2013. http://www.uscis.gov/eb-5centers.

United States Department of State. "Fees and Reciprocity Tables." Government website. March 1, 2013. http://travel.state.gov/visa/fees/fees_1341.html.

United States Department of State. "Treaty Countries." Government website. March 1, 2013. http://travel.state.gov/visa/fees/fees_3726.html.

United States Federal Bureau of Investigation (FBI). "Crime in the United States 2011." Government website. 2011. http://www.fbi.gov/about-us/cjis/ucr/crime-in-the-u.s/2011/crime-in-the-u.s.-2011.

Yale-Loehr, Stephen, Carolyn S. Lee, and Nicolai Hinrichsen. "EB-5 Immigrant Investors." In *Immigration Options for Investors and Entrepreneurs*, edited by Lincoln Stone et al. Washington, DC: American Immigration Lawyers Association, 2010.

Yale-Loehr, Stephen, Robert C. Divine, and Sonia Sujanani. "EB-5 I-829 RFEs: What Does USCIS Look For?" IIUSA Publication.

Endnotes

1. "Expediente Ciudadano," Consejo para la Ley y los Derechos Humanos (CLDH).
2. Yale-Loehr, Lee, and Hinrichsen, *Immigration Options for Investors and Entrepreneurs*, 61–77.
3. "Immigrant Investment Regional Centers," US Citizenship and Immigration Services (USCIS).
4. "Immigrant Investment Statistics," USCIS, 6.
5. "EB-5 Immigrant Investor Program Stakeholder Meeting September 15, 2011," USCIS, 13.
6. Joseph, "House Passes S. 3245, Sends 3 Year Reauthorization of EB-5 Regional Center Program to President Obama for Signature," September 13, 2012, http://iiusablog.org/government-affairs/house-passes-3-year-reauthorization-eb5-regional-center-program-sends-3245-president-signature/
7. Yale-Loehr, Divine, and Sujanani, *Immigration Options for Investors and Entrepreneurs*, 1–6.
8. Arias and Stone, Immigration Options for Investors and Entrepreneurs, 119–129.
9. "Immigrant Investment Statistics," USCIS, 1.

10. "Tax Revenue as Percentage of GDP," Organisation for Economic Co-operation and Development (© OECD 2012).
11. "Historical Exchange Rates," OANDA.
12. "Consumer Price Indexes for All Urban Consumers," US Bureau of Labor Statistics, 1.
13. "Crime in the United States 2011," US Federal Bureau of Investigation.
14. Ibid.
15. Ibid.
16. "Dictionary," Investopedia.
17. "Forms," USCIS.
18. "EB-5 Immigrant Investment Visa Program," USCIS.
19. Golbert and Golbert, *Immigration Options for Investors and Entrepreneurs*, 359–394.
20. Juceam, Sabagh, and Bacon, *Immigration Options for Investors and Entrepreneurs*, 265–277.
21. Ibid.
22. "Treaty Countries," US Department of State.
23. Ibid.

OPEN BOOK EDITIONS
A BERRETT-KOEHLER PARTNER

Open Book Editions is a joint venture between Berrett-Koehler Publishers and Author Solutions, the market leader in self-publishing. There are many more aspiring authors who share Berrett-Koehler's mission than we can sustainably publish. To serve these authors, Open Book Editions offers a comprehensive self-publishing opportunity.

A SHARED MISSION

Open Book Editions welcomes authors who share the Berrett-Koehler mission—Creating a World That Works for All. We believe that to truly create a better world, action is needed at all levels—individual, organizational, and societal. At the individual level, our publications help people align their lives with their values and with their aspirations for a better world. At the organizational level, we promote progressive leadership and management practices, socially responsible approaches to business, and humane and effective organizations. At the societal level, we publish content that advances social and economic justice, shared prosperity, sustainability, and new solutions to national and global issues.

Open Book Editions represents a new way to further the BK mission and expand our community. . We look forward to helping more authors challenge conventional thinking, introduce new ideas, and foster positive change.

For more information, see the Open Book Editions website:
http://www.iuniverse.com/Packages/OpenBookEditions.aspx

Join the BK Community! See exclusive author videos, join discussion groups, find out about upcoming events, read author blogs, and much more! http://bkcommunity.com/

www.ingramcontent.com/pod-product-compliance
Lightning Source LLC
Chambersburg PA
CBHW031051180526
45163CB00002BA/782